OVERCOMING *in* DIFFICULT *times*

Nora King

Melbourne, Florida USA

OVERCOMING IN DIFFICULT TIMES
by Nora King

Parsons Publishing House
P. O. Box 410063, Melbourne FL 32940 USA
www.ParsonsPublishingHouse.com
Info@ParsonsPublishingHouse.com

Publisher elects not to capitalize satan.

ISBN-13: 978-160273-118-9
ISBN-10: 1-60273=118-7
Library of Congress Control Number: 2020935341
Printed in the United States of America.
For World-Wide Distribution.

DEDICATION

This book is dedicated to my dad, The Reverend Loy G. Ramsey. It was my observing him when I was a young child that I wondered at his devotion to serving the Lord and his deep love for God.

Beginning in his young life, he overcame many obstacles. His mother, my grandmother after whom I was named, passed away when he was only 18 months old, which contributed in no small part to difficulties growing up. This experience made him mindful of expressing his care and love for his family. He always made sure his children—me, my brother Carlos, and my sisters, Kathy, and Paulette—were aware of his love and provision for us.

He served in the army during World War II and fought in fierce battles while stationed in France. At times, he would give us a glimpse into what he went through. I knew it weighed heavily on his mind.

Although his formal education was limited, he overcame this by receiving training in various skills through his veteran's benefits to help support his young family.

He was passionate about God and His Word. At the last church my dad pastored, he took a small group and cared for them diligently with his whole heart. At the time of his death, the church had grown considerably. Truly, he was a "shepherd" that loved the "sheep," and they loved him.

My dad gave me much more than provision; he gave me a heritage of love for God, the Bible, and family! For this, I am truly and forever thankful.

I was nineteen years old when my dad passed away, and it was devastating to me. I began my journey in life as an adult with a deep hurt in my heart and did not understand the things I am now sharing in this book. Consequently, I had many unanswered questions, pain, confusion, and even bitterness because my father, who had loved me and shown me the way, was no longer there for me. I followed in my dad's footsteps and surrendered my life to the Heavenly Father as my dad modeled.

That changed everything.

Loy Ramsey has been in heaven for many years, but his legacy lives on to this day.

TABLE OF CONTENTS

ACKNOWLEDGMENTS

Special thanks to those who assisted
in the editing of this book:

Katy Blackburn
Deborah Smallwood
Bill Buchanan
Anne Martin

INTRODUCTION

When you're in troubled times, remember—it's not the end. God has new beginnings for you. It's not time to give up or give in to your predicament. Move the mountain out of your way through God's never-changing Word and persistent, targeted prayer. James 5:16 in the Amplified Version says tremendous power (dynamic power) is released toward our problem when we sincerely pray and believe. There's power made available to blast through the most difficult situations one may face. In God, standing steadfast and immovable in the midst of difficulty is imperative.

But bad things do happen to good people, and sometimes we do not understand why. However, Scripture is full of guidance and direction while in adversity. In this book, I have set out to bring some understanding to help in troubled times.

> When you go through deep waters, I will be with you. When you go through rivers of difficulty, you will not drown. When you walk through the fire of oppression, you will not be burned up; the flames will not consume you (Isaiah 43:2, NLT).

God is with you today. You are not alone in your struggles. He will help you to overcome adversity. Hold onto His hand.

> We think you ought to know, dear brothers and sisters, about the trouble we went through in the province of Asia. We were crushed and overwhelmed beyond our ability to endure, and we thought we would never live through it. In fact, we expected to die. But as a result, we stopped relying on ourselves and learned to rely only on God, who raises the dead. And he **did** rescue us from mortal danger, and he **will** rescue us again. We have placed our confidence in him, and he **will continue** to rescue us (2 Corinthians 1:8-11, NLT, emphasis added).

Paul was in dire circumstances. It seemed like the end for him and beyond human ability to make it! This Scripture reveals that Paul had been rescued in his PAST, and he knew that God was delivering him from what he was going through IN THE PRESENT MOMENT. The apostle had faith and trusted God that He would do the same in the FUTURE. He didn't have to fear or wonder if the Lord would come through this time. We need to "cast our lot" in with Paul and believe that crushing—even overwhelming and brutal—circumstances will not be able to stop or defeat us because He is our Deliverer who rescues us out of all circumstances. Like Paul, think about your previous times of deliverance and victory over situations you experienced.

> For who are you, O great mountain [of human obstacles]? Before Zerubbabel [who with Joshua had led the return of the exiles from Babylon and was undertaking the rebuilding of the temple, before him] you shall become a plain [a mere [a]molehill]! (Zechariah 4:7, AMPC).

We also need this "can-do" attitude and scripturally speak aloud to the obstacles we face. As this Scripture references, we can face a mountain of human obstacles that overshadow us, and when we do, say this: "With God on my side, I will not be hindered or stopped in Jesus' great name!"

Obstacles to the left and right of us will be leveled as we trust, believe, and speak forth God's powerful promises and covenant. A covenant is a binding agreement between two parties. In this case, it is an agreement between you and the Father, sealed in Jesus' blood.

What a strong and powerful alliance! You and God are an unbeatable team. So, find in your Bible the covenant answers to your difficulty and do not be moved from that truth. Feelings, emotions, and circumstances must conform to the truth, and they will certainly align themselves with it. We may be staring at the "facts" before us, but the Word of God is the ultimate truth. Don't ever give up too soon!

Chapter 1

MY STORY OF OVERCOMING GREAT DIFFICULTY

As I am sharing the essential truths in this book, I know it is necessary to set up the following chapters by talking about my own life experiences and how they have shaped my life and given me a perspective that I would not otherwise have. So, let's begin.

My husband and I have two children, Laren and Marcus, whom we dearly love. We brought them up to live for the Lord and be guided by the truths of Scripture. Our family has always been loving, and it was important to me that my kids knew that we were thankful for them and recognized that they were gifts from God to us.

A Little Peek Into My Family

We had fun being together as my children were growing up. When they were younger, Friday nights were our family nights. We would order food—pizza, what else—their favorite! We would play games, rent videos, and listen to music—usually from the '60s—and dance up a storm! Many times, our daughter Laren, with her creative flair, would give us makeup and hair makeovers. Not only on me, but on her dad and even little brother Marcus, too. These were such good and rich times for us as a family. These are only a glimpse into a few of the warm memories that we shared as a family.

We went through the challenges of the teenage years, like all parents with kids do. But we had dedicated both Laren and Marcus to the Lord and trusted Him to see us through.

My son, Marcus, was a precious baby given to us by God, who was active and so full of energy. He grew to be witty, intelligent, and always full of questions! He changed our world!

Then the difficulties came as he entered his teenage years. We looked to the Lord for His wisdom and guidance.

In May 2005, my world came crashing down to never return to the "normal" we had enjoyed. Marcus passed away at 17 years of age. I was absolutely stunned and lost my equilibrium for living—feeling paralyzed and unsure that I could live life any longer. I know it was the prayers of the people that loved my husband, me, and our daughter that carried us in that dark night of our souls. It was God's Word that I had hidden in my heart that brought strength to me when I was at my weakest point. He was faithful to carry me through, and He brought a sustaining power that I had to have to strengthen me moment by moment, day by day.

It has been many years since my son's passing. I have not shared much publicly because it is too painful. However, I do feel that this is God's timing to share from my experience in order to minister to others; so, I am endeavoring to follow His leading. The Lord has allowed me the time I needed to get to this place.

On the day I was to plan Marcus' memorial service, I was driving with tears flowing so heavily I could barely see to drive. At that moment, Job 13:15 came from deep inside of me, and I said this Scripture out loud:

> "Though he slay me, yet will I trust in him"
> (Job 13:15).

I determined that day that I would not blame God; I would not become bitter or harbor unforgiveness in my heart against the One who had saved me, transformed my life, and had given me Marcus. Let me be clear, I don't think God "slayed" my son, but I identified with Job in stating his unwavering dedication to God even amid such upheaval in my life.

For some time after Marcus passed, I felt I could not even pray. I was so overcome with grief; all I could do was stand before the Lord, lift my hands, and worship. In total surrender to the Lord, in my brokenness, all I could do at that time was ask God to help me—help us—because I did not know how I could go on in life. Daily, His sustaining power was imparted.

> The thief cometh not, but for to steal, and to kill, and to destroy: I am come that they might have life, and that they might have it more abundantly (John 10:10).

The devil is the killer and destroyer. At first, I felt I couldn't go on, but then I would experience His comforting mercy and grace, pulling me up from the depths of despair. I began to rise up and practice the things I've shared in this book to overcome that great devastation. If it sustained and carried me, it will do the same for you because "God is no respecter of persons" (Acts 10:34).

Truly I felt like I was being raised from the ashes of a burnt-out hull. A new "plant" began to rise. It would not look the same nor think or see in the same ways—the plant was me. By living through the pain and anguish of my son's death, it allowed me to become much more aware of the pain and heartache of others. I was infused with great compassion—supernaturally—and a desire to help them by pointing them to hold to Jesus and His unchanging hand. He is willing and able to heal the brokenhearted and restore and take them from brokenness to wholeness.

> The Spirit of the Lord is upon me, because he hath anointed me to preach the gospel to the poor; he hath sent me to **heal the brokenhearted**, to preach **deliverance to the captives**, and **recovering of sight to the blind**, to **set at liberty them that are bruised** (Luke 4:18, emphasis added).

Jesus Christ gives this gospel message in its power to those who are broken and hurting—whether spiritually, emotionally, or even naturally. He provides healing to the brokenhearted. This promise is speaking of those who have been emotionally crushed by the circumstances of life. He gives us freedom and releases us from the prison and captivity that our deep wounds and sufferings have brought us. Jesus enables us to have blinders removed so we can see circumstances for what they really are. Finally, He has made the way to be liberated from brokenness because of the calamity we have experienced. We can be "bruised" because of the distress. This bruising is not literal, but an outward indicator of something that has deeply affected our lives. When allowed to work in and for us, the anointing upon Jesus Christ, our Lord, unshackles us from our pain and grief. I am a testimony of His faithfulness.

As I am writing this, Marcus has been in heaven for over several years now. That seems unimaginable! I still have sad moments and think of him daily, but I know reunion is coming. Marcus is with me now in my heart, and we will be together in the future. Because of this, I have great hope. Indeed the "healing balm of Gilead" has been applied to my broken heart and broken life. Because of this, things will never be the same, but my Lord and Savior Jesus Christ has walked with me every step of the way to bring comfort, peace, and strength.

Even though my son is gone from my life upon this Earth, it isn't final. I have the hope and assurance I will see him again—to be reunited in heaven where there will be no more separation nor parting. I give thanks to God that Marcus is in my future. As King David said when his own son had passed, "*I can't bring him back to me, but I can go where he is.*"

In this most challenging time of my life, Jesus has been faithful to me. He raised me up from this crushing and devastating time. I fully trust and lean on Him. I can say to you, whatever you are facing today, my God will sustain you. You, too, can overcome in your difficult time.

Your difficulties may be devastating and tragic, like mine, or maybe not. But I'm here to point the way to your ability to overcome through Jesus Christ. Whether facing severe problems or needing a way to confront life's daily demands, I believe the truths you read in this book will be illuminating and lead you into God's plan of blessing for your life.

CHAPTER 2

TRUST

I'm going to share things with you in this book that will help you overcome in difficult times. When you find yourself in a crisis, these are the things to consider carefully.

I wish I could honestly say that you will never face adversity, trouble, or trials, but that is simply not the truth. Anyone who indicates something like that is being dishonest. We must build our house on the firm foundation of the Word of God. Then in challenging times, it becomes our spiritual weaponry for fighting. The Bible is called the sword of the Spirit that we can use to counteract the enemy's plots and strategies and help us win the battle. Difficulty will come, so the question is: What are we going to do when it comes knocking at our door. I don't have an all-inclusive answer here; there's always more that can be said on the matter. However, what I'm going to impart to you are some things that God taught me personally and some things that He impressed upon me when I have ministered to individuals facing crucial situations.

When you find yourself in difficulty, lean on the Lord and expect Him to help you—expect Him to be there to take you through your challenges. God desires to support us; however, there are times He is unable because of the things we do to restrict Him—the things we're thinking, doing, and saying that actually tie His hands. We can do things that violate and counteract the truths of Scripture—not even realizing it—and stop the Lord from being able to bring answers to us.

> And he could there do no mighty work, save that he laid his hands upon a few sick folk, and healed them. And he marvelled because of their unbelief (Mark 6:5-6).

Mark, chapter six, records that Jesus could only help those with minor ailments. Why? Because of their unbelief. The unbelief of people limited God. He has set up laws or guidelines through which we may live and overcome. In the Old Testament, it says Israel limited God. When you find yourself in a formidable situation, **expect** God to make a way for you. To "expect" means to look forward, to anticipate, and to await. When you rely on His Word and trust Him, He will see you through because this is the way of belief—the way of faith. We don't need to try to figure it out. Just allow Him to do what you cannot.

We can count on the Lord. He never fails us, and He is faithful in every storm. Sometimes we can feel alone and isolated, but He has told us He will not abandon us as orphans. He will come alongside us. We have a loving, caring heavenly Father who isn't mad at us and doesn't leave us. This promise is essential to understand, but I am sad to say that I was unaware of this for many years. That's why I am sharing this truth here.

There have been times in my life when a crisis came, and one of the first things that came out of my mouth was, "God, I trust

You. I don't understand, but I will trust You anyway!" That means you place all of who you are in His hands—resting and leaning on the Lord. Trust Him in difficulty, and He will clear the way for you. Trust is a vital element in the life of a believer.

> "Trust in the Lord with all thine heart; and
> lean not unto thine own understanding"
> (Proverbs 3:5).

In Hebrew, the word "trust" comes from a term that means to wrestle. This definition refers to wrestling with our own self-reliance, our doubts, our fears, and our worries and then, totally placing ourselves in His hands, not giving way to human reasoning and emotions. That truly is a wrestling match! Human reasoning will cause you to lose heart, but trust and reliance on the Lord will help you move toward victory. Sometimes we try so hard to figure everything out on our own, spending countless hours stewing over it. Instead, we can lean on God's strong arms, and by faith, find and receive His answer and become steadfast. After you have wrestled fear and doubt out of the way, with your faith still intact, the path to sweet victory is before you! It requires patiently waiting for it.

I want to tell you a true story. When I was a child, I attended summer camp. The camp counselors would attempt to teach us individually how to swim. But, I would go to the corner of the pool and firmly plant myself there. The counselor would say, "Push off from the side of the pool and swim toward me." But I was cowering in the corner of the pool in fear and torment while saying, "No, no, no." There was absolutely no trust there at all. Fear had gripped me, and I became paralyzed.

This story is an example of how our walk with the Lord is at times. You can be in life's storms that are brewing all around, but Jesus, with His hands outstretched, bids you to rely on Him. He will hold you up and help you in the midst of the storm. But like me as a child, you stand in the corner full of fear and say you cannot. But the TRUTH is: yes, you can if you place your trust firmly in Him and allow Him to help you. Trust that when you launch out into the water, He's going to be there to hold you up. Jesus helped Peter when he stepped out of the boat, but Peter had to trust in the Lord. He was literally empowered to walk on water by Jesus! He will hold you up, too.

"What time I am afraid, I will trust in thee"
(Psalm 56:3).

Everyone deals with fear on some level. When fear pushes in on you, deliberately trust in the Lord and find Scriptures relating to your circumstance that you can believe in and speak aloud in the middle of seemingly devastating circumstances. Fear hinders you so that you are not able to go forward with life, and you remain stuck in the middle of the problem. But, He has made a way out of despair.

It has been my experience that even though fear is rising up in me, and my mind is telling me I'm going to fail—I won't make it, I have to go ahead and do what I fear. I don't give in to satan's lies. Then afterward I look back and see, because I was leaning on the Lord for strength, by faith, I made it, despite fearful thoughts and emotions. God doesn't give us fear, 2 Timothy 1:7 discloses:

"For God hath not given us the spirit of fear; but of power, and of love, and of a sound mind" (2 Timothy 1:7).

So, from where does fear come? The devil, for sure! Other factors can also play a part—our upbringing, surroundings, past teachings, and even our personality may have a role in it. Rise up and declare: "The Lord is on my side, and I will not fear!" It's your choice whether to fear or to reject fear. I make a choice: FAITH OVER FEAR!

"Preserve me, oh God, for in You do I put my trust" (Psalm 16:1).

Preserve me! If you think about the word "preserve," it means to protect, to keep, and to save. Cry out to God with these words: "Keep me, Lord; protect me, for I put my trust in You during these insurmountable troubles I am facing."

Many Christians do not understand this, but we are to rely on the Lord no matter in what situation we find ourselves, small or great. Some think they can only go to God for great needs or significant issues, but in every situation and circumstance, minute by minute, we can depend on Him daily. Let's include Him in our conversation, in our relationships, in our behavior, and especially in our problems. God never leaves us.

As you trust in the Lord, He will be your protector. Sometimes you cannot protect yourself, but He is willing and able, so rest and lay back into His unchanging arms!

"For God has said, 'I will never leave you; I will never abandon you'" (Hebrews 13:5, GNT).

He is ALWAYS with us! Maybe you've been left or abandoned in your life, possibly through childhood experiences with family or those close to you, or even through a marriage partner that abandoned you, and now you strive to trust, but it isn't easy for you. The Lord is not like humans who are weak at times and make mistakes; He is trustworthy. There have been times in my life that I have felt isolated, alone, and even misunderstood as a woman in ministry, especially in the early days. In my circles, it was not as acceptable for women to be in ministry as it is today. In many ways, I felt like a pioneer, even though many women have gone before me! There were times I faced hardships and hindrances and had to remind myself that God was with me. He called me and was working in and through me—my constant companion who would never abandon me. Then as I ministered the Word to people, it was the Lord who touched people and changed lives despite my circumstances.

When my father—who was a Baptist pastor and a wonderful dad—went to heaven, I felt utterly orphaned. For a young woman, it was a foreboding emotional experience. But in time, God revealed Himself to me through my loss in a new, fresh, and amazing way. Our heavenly Father will NEVER desert us. In your loss, He will remain faithful to you and be by your side to comfort and strengthen you.

"The thief does not come except to
steal, and to kill, and to destroy"
(John 10:10a, NKJV).

As John 10:10 states, the enemy's plan is to bring decimation and destruction into your life, but your reliance on the Lord will uphold you and bring you into His abundant life. This

Scripture refers to the devil's strategy or plan against us. Don't allow the enemy to lie to you and convince you the stealing, killing, and destroying is God's work! We can judge the situation by what's happening—killing, stealing, and destroying is not of God, but the devil! This Scripture verse continues and tells us what God's work is:

> "I came that they may have and enjoy life, and have it in abundance [to the full, till it overflows]" (John 10:10b, AMP).

God wants us to have a good, full, and enriching life. This scriptural reference defines what the devil is doing and also what the Father wants to do in our lives. Years ago, this was a major revelation to me. I would intermingle Scripture and become totally confused; however, the truth of the Scripture brings freedom from confusion and understanding in the ways of God. The understanding I received is a divine mystery that was revealed to me!

I began to be a student of the Word and read the Bible for myself and listened to people who taught the Bible. There's a disclosure of truth that comes forth as you are growing in the Word and as you grow in your walk with God—it's line upon line and precept upon precept. In other words, we grow little by little. So, understanding who is behind destructive acts and who is bringing blessing into your life is vitally important in your growth process! Do not try to rely on your own human reasoning and emotions because you will be misled. Trust God by believing His Word, the Bible—His promises to us!

> "Blessed [with spiritual security] is the man who believes and trusts in and relies on the Lord, and whose hope and confident expectation is the Lord. For he will be [nourished] like a tree planted by the waters, that spreads out its roots by the river; and will not fear the heat when it comes; but its leaves will be green and moist. And it will not be anxious and concerned in a year of drought nor stop bearing fruit (Jeremiah 17:7-8, AMP).

When the "heat is on" in your life and satan has turned up his destructive fires, allow the Holy Spirit to give you the strength to stand and overcome as you trust and rely on Him. Scripture is referred to as the "water of the Word." As you stay connected to Scripture and it is before your eyes and reigning in your heart, you will be watered, refreshed, and cleansed. This dependence on the Word will deepen your *root system* in God and allow you to stand firm when the heat is turned up in your life.

CHAPTER 3

PERSONAL EVALUATION

When you find yourself in a season of trouble, it's time to ask yourself some specific questions. **First question**: Could this be a result of any wrongdoing on my part—my irresponsibility, lack of wisdom, or sin—thereby opening a door to the enemy? When I'm facing adversity, this is something I look at personally. You may have to do some soul searching and consideration when you are experiencing difficult times. If it is a result of you opening the door for something to happen, consider this:

> "If we confess our sins, he is faithful and just to forgive us our sins, and to cleanse us from all unrighteousness" (1 John 1:9).

This verse is written to the believer, not an unbeliever. When you confess your sin, you are cleansed and forgiven, putting you in a position for the Holy Spirit to help you deal with your problem and ultimately overcome it.

> "There is therefore now no condemnation to them which are in Christ Jesus, who walk not after the flesh, but after the Spirit" (Romans 8:1).

If you feel you've opened the door to personal attack, receive forgiveness, and then you MUST move on past it. Do not continue to beat yourself up or live under condemnation after repenting to the Lord. You must drop your mistake (as God does) and move forward toward your victory. Once we confess and ask for forgiveness, the Lord doesn't remember it—it's gone! So, we should strive to do the same by faith. I will say that our sin can have consequences involving our relationships with others, but to God, you are cleansed and forgiven—the "slate is wiped clean!"

The **second question** to ask: Is God trying to get my attention for a change and a new direction? This question is crucial. God spoke to Elijah, the prophet, and told him to go to the Brook Cherith where the ravens would bring his daily provision. His provision lasted for a while; food and water were always available for him. Then one day, the brook dried up, and Elijah had to go a different direction for his supply—God had another way to provide for him. When you get in the middle of a crisis, you have to ask yourself, "Do I need a new direction? Do I need to make adjustments? Is the Lord trying to give me further guidance?" Don't decide this on your own; be led by the Holy Spirit.

The **third question** to ask: Is this a demonic attack? Has the enemy launched a barrage against me? Satan clearly wants to stop God's plan in your life any way he can. I'll say more about this in Chapter 12.

Consider also that this could be a combination of all these things. God's residing wisdom will help you discern the truth. If you have been irresponsible and allowed an opening in your life to the devil, you can close that door! Scripture says to give no place (no toehold) to the devil. Even a crack in that door allows him to enter; however, knowledge is power, and you can cut the enemy's encroachment off.

When your needs are not being met, these questions I've mentioned can guide you in taking a step of faith into God's plan—by thinking about your situation and finding His solution, provision, and next move. As you look over these things and ponder them, I pray the Holy Spirit will enlighten you and begin to speak directly and specifically to you.

Let me say this: you can be introspective to the point of damaging your faith. I'm not indicating that here. Once you understand the blockage, deal with it and go on. Living in regret will only hold you back. Learn what God desires for you to see and understand, then listen and obey. Don't be like the Israelites and keep going around the same mountain over and over. Moses said to Israel: "*You have been going around THIS mountain long enough.*" If this is where you are in your life, make a decision to break out of the pattern, moving on into productivity and fruitfulness.

CHAPTER 4

FEED YOUR FAITH

The other day when a person called and left a prayer request—just like hundreds of people do all the time—I felt drawn to say to him, "Whatever you do, find someone to preach faith to you." It's not time to listen to eschatology, even though we all love to learn about the end times as we look forward to Jesus' return. It is time to allow someone to preach faith to you. Let them preach and preach and preach until it drives out unbelief and fear and imparts overcoming faith! We must settle down and allow the Word of God to deal with circumstances—one by one—while it chases out doubt and creates God-thoughts in your mind concerning His provision. Then allow faith and confidence in His promises to flourish and bring strength to stand against the obstacles that are coming your way.

I remember someone told me they had received one of my messages that inspired their faith, and they gave it to a family member who was suffering through severe depression and strong demonic attack. The woman had lost a lot of weight, couldn't function on her job, and wasn't able to sleep. The person told the family member to listen to the message, and she did. Then she listened to it again and again. She didn't stop listening to it for a prolonged period of time. The person who gave her my message came back and conveyed to me that this family member was totally healed and delivered of the depression/oppression that had attacked her. Why? Because it was the truth of Scripture that was faith-inspiring. It spoke to her saying she could overcome her circumstances. She was going to make it, and the devil was not going to destroy her life! There's "devil-busting" power in Scripture!

So, find messages that preach prevailing faith to you, and if you have to listen to it over and over again, just do it—whatever it takes. You might say, "Well, I listened to it one time." Have you changed yet? No? Then keep listening to it! Just keep listening to it until it sinks into your spirit and mind and changes your attitude and the spirit world around you. Begin to think about God's solution! Talk about His solutions, and then act upon them.

"And this is the victory that has overcome the world —our faith" (1 John 5:4, NKJV).

I follow this instruction myself when I have challenging situations. I want someone preaching and teaching the Word of God to me and imparting truths that help me see God has made a way to overcome the adversity. I tell myself, "I am going to get through, and I am going to go to the other side!" The waters may be rough, but get in the boat because you're going to the other side! We must have hope, faith, and courage. I may have heard a Scripture before, but I will listen until it drives fear, unbelief, and defeat from me and gives me victory over circumstances.

What you allow yourself to see and hear is critical when in the middle of difficulties. Don't listen to people in your life who rob you of hope, courage, and faith. I'm sorry to say that it seems there may be more people in this category than those who impart faith.

> Casting down imaginations, and every high thing that exalteth itself against the knowledge of God, and **bringing into captivity every thought** to the obedience of Christ (2 Corinthians 10:5, emphasis added).

We must stop thinking about, dwelling on, and being fixated on the difficulties around us. We also must stop talking about our crisis—repeating it over and over to whoever will listen. Some people say they believe in God's promises one minute, and the next thing out of their mouth, they are rehearsing their crisis again for the tenth time! Their problem is all they think and talk about. You can be released from the crisis by placing God's Word in your mouth and allowing it to supernaturally "slash" through the problem—remember: the Word is called the sword of the Spirit! With faith in your heart and God's Word in your mouth, speak to your mountain and command it to align with God's promises!

My husband and I would not be in the position that we are in today as pastors if we had given in every time the devil came to say he was going to destroy us or that we were not going to make it. Many times, it looked to be disaster and failure, but we chose to believe God's call on our lives, His assignment for us, and His promise and provision. Then, we made a decision to talk about this instead of how circumstances appeared to be. You must learn to stir yourself in the faith of God and put His promises in your heart, in your mouth, and in your mind by thinking and meditating upon them. And if a destructive thought comes, what do you do? You cast it down in Jesus' name, and you refuse to receive the thought. It is important to fight through with your faith and not settle for the state of affairs as they are! Then answer back with your promise from Scripture.

As I said, people can be deceptively used by the enemy to attack your belief in the Bible. But, be like David when his jealous brother tried to discourage him from taking on the giant, Goliath. David didn't respond to the negative remarks of his brother, Eliab, but turned from him and began to talk to others who would listen about his thoughts and ideas on overcoming the giant. David took the giant's head off and won victory for Israel! So, turn from the faith-robbers and continue speaking God's promises and take the "giant" problems you're facing and decapitate them! I realize many Christians, just like Eliab, may not understand they are acting to overthrow another's faith. Many times, they are not evil people, just people who do not understand scriptural principles.

> Therefore whosoever heareth these sayings of mine, and doeth them, I will liken him unto a wise man, which built his house upon a rock: And the rain descended, and the floods came, and the winds blew, and beat upon that house; and it fell not: for it was founded upon a rock (Matthew 7:24-25).

Storms come into everyone's life. We must secure ourselves by building our lives on a firm foundation of Scripture. When turbulence is surrounding us, our house will stand securely if we deliberately and continuously act on God's powerful, sustaining promises. He will never let you sink. You will be upheld and kept above the fray. We have to be aware of this truth when we begin to see those around us failing. Make sure you keep your eyes on Jesus, not people. We cannot have a full understanding of what's going on between others and their Lord and their foundation, but we can take care of knowing that our own foundation in God's Word has anchored us in the midst of the storm.

You cannot think and meditate on crisis, difficulty, and adversity, constantly rehearsing it over and over, and then expect to overcome. There are laws of the kingdom to which we must adhere. When you put the Word of God in motion, it begins to change your circumstances; it begins to rearrange things for you. God's Word is not natural, but supernatural, and it begins to move and attract answers toward us as if it had a magnetic pull! You put the Bible in motion by your beliefs, your words, and your actions. I have seen it work many times in my life. It's too late to tell me it doesn't work; it's already been proven in my life—it works!

> "Heaven and earth shall pass away, but my words shall not pass away" (Matthew 24:35).

When distress comes, are we going to act or react? What will we say? Will we get bitter? Or will we get stronger? Will we give up, or will we fight? Those are genuine issues and real considerations, aren't they? I cannot answer these things for you, and you cannot answer for me. We must look inside ourselves and make necessary corrections in our course to determine a different and biblical outcome in our lives.

Chapter 5

FASTING IN DIFFICULT TIMES

When you are facing hard times and don't know what to do, considering a fast would be wise. There's a time to celebrate, feast, and enjoy God's goodness; there is also a time to fast by shutting down your regular schedule and activities to be with the Lord. Not having the responsibilities of meal preparation, etc., allows you more time for specific focus. Fasting doesn't make you holy, just obedient. It aligns you to be open to hear the voice of the Lord more clearly, as well as it releases God's power to battle against the demonic unseen realm.

> Is this not the fast that I have chosen: to loose the bonds of wickedness, to undo the heavy burdens, to let the oppressed go free, and that you break every yoke? (Isaiah 58:6, NKJV).

In Christendom, fasting is a lost directive to many people. It isn't talked about, understood, or practiced very much. Fasting is not something that you only do at the first of the year. It is a tradition for our church to fast in January—a godly tradition and collective effort. However, there are times of crisis in your own life when you should determine to fast. You can ask your spouse or a friend to join you, but don't be dependent upon someone else. Assume your responsibility and go after breakthroughs and answers.

Fasting—the act of going without food—causes you to deprive your physical body of so much attention. Your body may say, "Give me my fried chicken and coconut pie! I want…I want…" Sometimes, I feel that way when I fast! Your body is crying out all the time, and you say, like a true southerner, "No, you aren't getting fried chicken. No food for you today."

Some think it's fanatical to fast, but I assure you, it's not; a biblical fast is appropriate. Fasting is spoken of in both the New and Old Testaments. Power is generated in the spirit realm when we purposefully control and take charge of our bodies and our physical appetites. Spend time with God and seek Him at those times when you would be preparing and eating a meal. Set this time apart for fasting and don't eat for a day or two or however long you choose. Make sure you read the Bible during this time.

I'm not going to get into the different kinds of fasts here—if you want more information on fasting, find a scripturally balanced author with titles on the subject. There are, however, important things to know: be sure to drink plenty of water on your fast and don't fast too many days in a way that would harm your body. Those directives are worth mentioning because sincere people can be extreme without realizing it.

Isaiah says that one thing fasting accomplishes is to "loose the bands of wickedness" (Isaiah 58:6). If you're in a crisis or in distress, with wicked spirits attached to your situation, the Bible says that the chains of wickedness (fetters) are broken by fasting. Fasting allows the power of those things to be broken and destroyed supernaturally.

"To undo the heavy burdens...and that you break every yoke" (Isaiah 58:6, NKJV).

God's fast is not just going without food, but it deals with the things that hinder and bind us, allowing us to get to the heart of the matter.

To "hinder" is to box you in or obstruct and keep you from overcoming the circumstances before you. When you are facing difficult times, there can be a mental weight and pressure on you. There can also be stress attached to what you're going through. This Scripture indicates that the bondage and weight will be lifted, the oppressed or discouraged shall go free, and the yoke (fetters, restrictions) will be broken off your life and situation.

God wants us to live daily in the peace that surpasses human comprehension, without frustration, anxiety, or torment. Fasting will help us achieve freedom from the pressures of life through Christ. Interestingly, the words "break every yoke" means to root out. Some things may need to be uprooted in your life. For us to have a beautiful garden, weeds have to be pulled and removed to enjoy the beauty. The same is true in our lives—some intrusions have to be eliminated.

> Which he wrought in Christ, when he raised him from the dead, and set him at his own right hand in the heavenly places, far above all principality, and power, and might, and dominion, and every name that is named, not only in this world, but also in that which is to come (Ephesians 1:21).

There is an angelic realm that is more real than what we can see and are experiencing right now, and things are occurring in this realm even when we cannot detect it. As we fast, angels in this heavenly realm are released to work on our behalf—the book of Daniel speaks of this. There is also a demonic kingdom with demonic forces that are just as real and active in the earth. Luke 10:19 says we, as God's people, have authority over the devil and his forces through the name of Jesus. Add to this authority by using God's Word, prayer, and fasting. How powerful! God didn't leave us on the earth unprepared to deal with our own issues without His supernatural provision. He reveals Himself to us in the Old Testament as Jehovah Jireh—our provider. But there are many who are unknowledgeable concerning this vital truth. Fasting is a spiritual weapon for God's people. Just as a soldier goes into a battle with his weapon drawn, we must be prepared for any crisis by using all the available spiritual weaponry given to us by God Himself (Ephesians 6:13-17).

"As they ministered to the Lord, and fasted, the Holy Ghost said, Separate me Barnabas and Saul for the work whereunto I have called them" (Acts 13:2).

The Holy Spirit spoke to the saints of old as they worshipped, prayed, and fasted. What a winning combination! God can speak to you as you separate yourself to pray and fast while seeking Him. You don't have to manufacture the voice of God. You don't have to act like you heard Him speak to you when you didn't, but inwardly hearing God's voice is actually available, guiding you during the fast. They ministered to the Lord and fasted, and the Holy Ghost spoke to them. Ministering to the Lord is worship. So, as they were praying, fasting, and worshipping, the Holy Spirit began to instruct them and give clear, concise direction and guidance. I have found that at the end of my fasting time, when I am more sensitive to the Lord, He can bring enlightenment to me. By that time, the clutter in my life surrounding the situation is sufficiently removed from blocking a God-centered view.

"Jesus Christ the same yesterday, and to day, and for ever" (Hebrews 13:8).

There have been many times when I've been on a fast, and the Holy Spirit impressed or spoke things to me. I remember years ago when we first started our church, and my husband and I were in a time of prayer and fasting. We desperately needed the Lord's guidance because we didn't have sufficient finances, a building, or people! We are an interdenominational church, not part of a specific denomination, so there wasn't anywhere we could turn to for help but the Lord!

We knew we had a divine call from God, and we were willing to follow Him despite everything that was stacked against us. As we ended our fast, we were getting close to home, and the Spirit of God flooded the car; we both were very aware of His presence at the same time. When we went into the house, Ed went downstairs to his study, and I went upstairs to the bedroom. As I got into the room, the Lord began to speak several things to me. One of the things He distinctly revealed to me was that He wanted to use my hands to bring healing to people, and suddenly oil appeared in the palms of my hands. You may think that's flaky (I've seen people do all kinds of strange things myself, so I don't want to sound that way), but I had oil in the palms of my hands—I couldn't make that happen. It was a supernatural event.

Again, this came at the end of my time of fasting. We were facing difficult times because we were trying to establish a church for God, and there were obstructions on every side. The enemy came against us using people to try to hinder and stop us. It was a very trying time, to say the least. We know people are not our enemy—it's the devil behind them—but people sure listen to the devil! My flesh wanted to get in their face and say, "Devil, come out!" Of course, I wouldn't actually do that, but I did bind his power operating through them behind the scenes and didn't just stand still and allow it!

When you're praying and fasting, you need to be open to hearing the voice of the Lord, as well as knowing how to receive insight from Him. Be open and willing to listen to God's direction and not your own willful desires. During fasting, when we're in a crisis, we may want to hear a certain thing so badly that sometimes we aren't as open to receive what the Spirit of God is impressing on us. We must be open and teachable to discern His guidance and leading instead of having our own way.

As you're reading the Bible, allow Scripture to speak to you as you fast and pray. Then pray in the Spirit (in tongues). The Bible says in 1 Corinthians 14 that when you pray in the Spirit, you pray forth divine secrets and mysteries:

> For one who speaks in an unknown tongue does not speak to people but to God; for no one understands him or catches his meaning, but by the Spirit he speaks mysteries [secret truths, hidden things] (1 Corinthians 14:2, NKJV).

What is a mystery or a secret? It's something about which you have no knowledge. A mystery is something hidden that needs to be revealed. The Lord wants us to have His inside information! (For more on spiritual language, refer to Chapter 11.)

We are all busy and have hectic schedules, but understand that there are times when you have to settle down and make yourself be silent. Being quiet and still before the Lord is vital in being able to receive communication from the Holy Spirit. Often, we drown out God's voice by pleading and asking instead of allowing Him to reveal these secrets and mysteries.

"Be still, and know that I am God"
(Psalm 46:10).

A point I want to make is "be still...and know." If you do all the talking in prayer, you will not be able to receive God's wisdom and knowledge. Hearing God's voice only through what you feel and see can be very deceptive. I'm not saying that when the Holy Spirit manifests Himself, you cannot feel emotions. Certainly, you can, but if you're relying only on your senses, you can be misled. As you are still and quiet, God uses that time to implant knowledge inside you.

"For we walk by faith, not by sight"
(2 Corinthians 5:7).

Human Reasoning

"But ye have an unction from the Holy One, and
ye know all things" (1 John 2:20).

As you fast, you need to pray and calm yourself; listen for the Lord, and don't try to figure things out with human reasoning.

The Bible says an anointing that comes from God abides (lives) inside of you. It's from the Holy One and gives you the ability to "know all things." There are so many situations where we find ourselves when we have no idea what we should do. That's when you can, and should, rely on the Holy Spirit in you. This reliance must be developed, so I'm not suggesting instantaneous spiritual growth. No, it comes little by little. Relying on the Holy Spirit when things are less complicated in your life will enable you to grow and develop beyond your current spiritual level. Then when difficulties come to overwhelm, you have matured in discerning God's voice and are more confident. No matter if you are a babe in Christ or a mature Christian, we all grow and continue growing. None of us have arrived; we just keep on advancing and stretching!

Relying on the Holy Spirit does not negate godly counsel. The Bible tells us to avail ourselves of sound advice at times. It can be beneficial for you to seek out godly counsel, but you will want to make sure your counselor knows and practices the Bible—seasoned, proven and successful in their service to the Lord. Advisors need to offer biblical advice, not their own opinions. However, nothing will replace your personal commitment to praying, worshipping, and fasting.

Scriptural fasting will open up stable spiritual streams in our lives that some would not know about or even consider. Christians have fasting as a mighty weapon in our arsenal; we would all do well to practice it on a regular basis.

CHAPTER 6

PRAYER OF PETITION

Another thing to consider when you are going through a crisis is to make a prayer of petition. The prayer of petition is a specific kind of prayer. All Scriptures noted in this chapter can be used in your petition if you wish.

Don't Worry—Pray

"Do not be anxious about anything, but in every situation, by prayer and petition, with thanksgiving, present your requests to God" (Philippians 4:6, NIV).

Instead of fretting or worrying over a situation, seek the Lord's plan by finding the Scriptures that give you the promise. Then, bring your specific request before God with faith in your heart, knowing He is willing to change things. A prayer of petition is making a request to the Lord for a definite need. Whether it's your family, home, loss, or whatever—it's a change that is desired. Write it down as an explicit prayer request. On the prayer petition, have a place for the date so you will able to look back at it to see answers given to you by the Lord and to encourage yourself through it.

I want to impress upon you when you make a specific prayer petition, remain open to the Holy Spirit. If you want a red car, that is okay. But what if God wanted to give you a great deal on a black car? Are you open to it? Of course, this is a simple, natural example, but it demonstrates the point. I always try to tell people to allow God to work on your behalf when making your petition. For example, if you ask me to agree with you for a spouse and you want him/her to have certain qualities, such as looking a specific way and having a particular personality—it's wonderful that you have been that definite. Consider sometimes that all the details may not work out precisely in that way. You want to be attracted to whoever you marry, but sometimes we can be over the top with specifics to the point we miss a God-opportunity because we are not reasonable.

Generally speaking regarding marriage, if you are older and single, the "field" narrows, and a person may not be the exact image you wanted. People have come to me about things such as this saying, "He/she is just not the type of person I prayed about." I then respond, "You might need to rethink and ask yourself: Do they love God? Are they living a godly lifestyle? Do they love you? Are you compatible?" I've then seen them let their guard down and enter the relationship only to find they have much more in common with the person than they thought, and they fall in love with them. When we are no longer young, we can carry extreme expectations from our youth! After all, we are not perfect, and neither will others be flawless. His plan will be the best for you. Our subject isn't marriage, but this is useful information!

On your prayer petition, write down what you need and desire, then add the Scriptures that give you the promise. Again, throughout this chapter, I am providing you with a few

Scriptures to record on your petition. Begin with Matthew 18:19, which is to be used when asking another person to agree with you concerning your petition. At the end of this chapter, I have included a copy of a prayer petition I developed.

Agreement on Your Prayer Petition

Harmonizing in your hearts releases tremendous spiritual power. Unity brings God's favor and anointing. The Bible says the anointing destroys yokes—things that hinder and bind up your answer are annihilated. If a person doesn't understand or come into agreement with you, then find someone who understands biblical principles and ask them to agree with you concerning your prayer requests.

This is something my husband and I have practiced many times over the years concerning home, family, material items, ministry, etc. Do you have needs and difficulties in your life? Then develop a prayer petition. If you're married, have your spouse agree with you; if you're not married, find a prayer partner who can agree and harmonize with you concerning your request.

> Again I tell you, if two of you on earth agree (harmonize together, make a symphony together) about whatever [anything and [a]everything] they may ask, it will come to pass and be done for them by My Father in heaven (Matthew 18:19, AMPC).

Of course, what you ask God for needs to be godly and scriptural—not sinful, morally wrong, or evil!

Faith to Believe

"Therefore I say unto you, what things soever ye desire, when ye pray, believe that ye receive them, and ye shall have them" (Mark 11:24).

After you pray, it is important to believe that what you have asked for is already yours. You must receive or "take" by faith what God has given to you. That is what the word "receive" means in this Scripture: take.

Isaiah said, "Who shall believe the report of the Lord?" Many explain it away, disregard it, or overlook it, but actively choosing to believe God's Word and what He said will transform your world and bring about needed change in your life!

Some have asked me, what if it isn't God's will for me? I believe in this case the Lord would reveal it and you would comply and receive something better for yourself. I believe God leaves certain things in our lives up to us.

There's Power in the Name of Jesus

"Whatever you ask the Father in My name, He will give you" (John 16:23, NKJV).

When we ask anything of the Father, we're instructed to pray in Jesus' name. Jesus went to Calvary to redeem us. He stripped satan of authority and empowered us by giving us authority as believers through the mighty name of Jesus. Doors can open, and alignment can begin.

Thank God

"With thanksgiving, continue to make your [specific] requests known to God" (Philippians 4:6, AMP).

This verse tells us that when we bring our prayer petition back to the Lord, we continue to thank Him for it. We don't need to continue to ask—you've already done that.

Making a Prayer Petition:

1) Date your petition.
2) Write the Scripture references on your petition.
3) Mention your need to God.
4) Read your Scriptures aloud.
5) Agree in prayer.
6) Both sign the petition.
7) Anytime you think about it later on, thank God for it.
8) As you continue to thank God for your need being met, you can pray in the Spirit about it, as well.

If you prayerfully agreed, the Bible says, "WHEN you pray, believe that you receive." Doing this requires what some may call radical faith!

Seeing the Unseen

"'Call to Me, and I will answer you, and show you great and mighty things, which you do not know'" (Jeremiah 33:3, NKJV).

The New Living translation says, "I will show you remarkable secrets you do not know about things to come." There are secrets God desires to reveal and bring to us, but it's our responsibility to tap into it. "Call to Me—ask Me, and I will answer you." The Lord takes it a step further. After we ask, then, in time, He will begin to bring revelation and insight about your situation that you had no way of naturally knowing. We most likely wouldn't receive this disclosure if we didn't ask Him!

He will supernaturally disclose to you things beyond human understanding. He wants to make known to us "inside" information and not leave us in the dark or limping along in our problems.

I believe one reason we don't hear God could be because we're too busy worrying, fretting, and wrestling with our problem instead of giving it to God by faith and resting in His ability to bring it to pass and show us things to come!

I have heard people say they have asked God for things, but He didn't answer them. That is a misunderstanding of a scriptural truth. The Bible says to ask Him—call on Him, and He WILL answer you. So, use your prayer petition to overcome in this life when you need something to break through and come to pass in your life.

*A copy of this petition can be downloaded at www.redemptionchurch.com.

Prayer of Petition

Date: ____________

My Request:

Scriptures That Give Me the Promise:

For with God, nothing shall be impossible (Luke 1:37).
With men this is impossible, but with God all things are possible. (Matthew 19:26)

I believe I receive when I pray. (Mark 11:24)

____________ Signed ____________ Signed

CHAPTER 7

GOD'S PROTECTION

Another thing to consider in difficult times is that God's protection and upholding power has been made available to us.

> No weapon formed against you shall prosper, and every tongue which rises against you in judgment you shall condemn. This is the heritage of the servants of the Lord, and their righteousness is from Me," says the Lord (Isaiah 54:17, NKJV).

Weapons are formed to work against God's people, but they do not have to advance against you and win. Notice this: *every tongue that is raised against me in judgment, I will condemn.* At times, I have been going about my business and impressed to pray this verse. There could be malicious talk or scheming against you, and you may not have a natural understanding of it, but if God impresses you with this verse (or another)—speak it out loud and stand on the promise—follow that leading.

Confessing "no weapon formed against me" is an act of pushing back, fighting back—not against a person, but against the spirit behind a person's actions coming against you. Do not allow their schemes to come to fruition. Believe God to deal with them while they're trying to hinder with their words of cursing! Even though they are possibly plotting against you, trying to destroy you, speak out loud: "No weapon formed against me will prosper." Then no word that is spoken against you shall ultimately prosper or flourish if you understand your protection in Christ. There is a forming of words to create an atmosphere to bind you, but you can block it and stop it with your own spiritual actions. Whether you know something specific or not, know this biblical truth and use it as part of your weaponry to fight back. As you stand on this compelling truth, there is power released on your behalf to bring down the hindrances and destroy the curse. I'm not indicating paranoia—that everyone's against you—I'm talking about legitimate attacks.

"Thou preparest a table before me in the presence of mine enemies" (Psalm 23:5).

People can choose to make themselves your enemy. Look forward to sitting down at the bountiful table that God prepares just for you and enjoy His blessings as your enemies look on! Believe and receive this promise without malice and hatred in your heart toward any person. You cannot have animosity in your heart, or God's Word won't work for you. Keep a right attitude! Pray that God will deal with them and help them see how the devil is using them. Weapons and hindrances are pulled down in Jesus' name! Mercy for people is a good thing—but not on the devil! If people refuse to acknowledge the issue, you continue to stand on your covenant promise.

"Dearly beloved, avenge not yourselves, but rather give place unto wrath: for it is written, Vengeance is mine; I will repay, saith the Lord" (Romans 12:19).

Don't try to get revenge against another person. You will get in trouble with the Lord. God has ways of dealing with them; leave it in His hands.

> He who dwells in the secret place of the Most High shall remain stable and fixed under the shadow of the Almighty [Whose power no foe can withstand]. I will say of the Lord, He is my Refuge and my Fortress, my God; on Him I lean and rely, and in Him I [confidently] trust! For [then] He will deliver you from the snare of the fowler and from the deadly pestilence. [Then] He will cover you with His pinions, and under His wings shall you trust and find refuge; His truth and His faithfulness are a shield and a buckler. You shall not be afraid of the terror of the night, nor of the arrow (the evil plots and slanders of the wicked) that flies by day, Nor of the pestilence that stalks in darkness, nor of the destruction and sudden death that surprise and lay waste at noonday. A thousand may fall at your side, and ten thousand at your right hand, but it shall not come near you (Psalm 91:1-7, AMPC).

This Scripture reveals that when we abide and live in God's presence, we will be secure and rest in Him, and the enemy cannot stand against us successfully. We are to talk about how the Lord is our refuge and fortress of protection, affirming our total reliance and dependence on Him. We are told God will save us from the trap the devil lays before us. There is protection in His presence. He places His shield around us, and we become walled in from destruction and so much more.

Falling by the wayside may happen to others around you, but danger is not coming near you. What magnificent promises we have to lay hold of in difficult times! I encourage you to read these passages over and over in Psalm 91.

Winning Over Satan

"O my God, I trust in thee…let not mine enemies triumph over me" (Psalm 25:2).

When doubtful thoughts come, or contrary words want to roll off your lips concerning your circumstances, allow Scriptures, with spiritual power encapsulated, to flow from your mouth to counteract the enemy's work. Plead the blood of Jesus over your life and speak: "He always causes me to succeed and have victory in each situation through Christ Jesus and will not allow my enemies to triumph over me."

"This know also, that in the last days perilous times shall come" (2 Timothy 3:1).

We are in perilous times that are full of danger, stress, and hardship. But the Lord delivers His people out of these situations if we have dynamic faith in our heart and rely on Him to clear the way for us. In the times we are in, people are facing increased difficulties. Things wear at us little by little. Scripture tells us that the strategy of the enemy in the last days is to wear out and wear down the saints of God.

> And he shall speak great words against the most High, and shall wear out the saints of the most High, and think to change times and laws: and

> they shall be given into his hand until a time and
> times and the dividing of time (Daniel 7:25).

This wearing away process has to do with imperceptibly eroding a little at a time. No one knows it is happening. The devil is very cunning in that this process happens so gradually; many do not realize they're in his vice until they are vanquished, reduced, and significantly weakened. Take action God's way, and know God has provided protection for you!

CHAPTER 8

HEARING GOD IN TIMES OF CRISIS

Look Up

> And the Lord said to Abram, after Lot had separated from him: "Lift your eyes now and look from the place where you are—northward, southward, eastward, and westward; for all the land which you see I give to you and your descendants forever. And I will make your descendants as the dust of the earth; so that if a man could number the dust of the earth, then your descendants also could be numbered. Arise, walk in the land through its length and its width, for I give it to you" (Genesis 13:14-17, NKJV).

First, Abraham had to separate himself from those that sidetracked him—his own family. Of course, most people don't have to make this kind of radical decision with their families, but he did. We should all distance ourselves from people and situations that impede our spiritual progress in following Jesus Christ. Not with a "holier than thou" attitude, of course—we are to love people!

Abraham was told to lift up his head and look at something other than the circumstances surrounding him in the place he was living. His current situation looked like this: he had no children, although he was told by God that he would have many descendants. Abraham had to look past the conflicting thoughts and the reality around him and lock his eyes squarely on God, believing that He was able to do what He promised—what was impossible with men.

In the place where you are, in the middle of difficult times, lift your head to heaven and see something beyond your surroundings. So many things and people are vying for or competing for your attention. They try to ensnare you in the situation you find yourself so you will take your eyes off the Lord's promises and the possibility to do amazing things in your life.

Seeing the Invisible

When God gives an assignment to me, I must get my focus off the matter at hand, off my inabilities and insecurities, and I must place faith in His promises and focus on the direction He has given to me. At that point, I can move forward. I've had to do this many times.

During times of hardness or harsh conditions, keeping the sweet aroma of victory before you is imperative. Endurance doesn't mean giving in or putting up with your situation, but it does mean doing what it takes to fight the good fight of faith to obtain the victory before you. Numerous people fold at the first glimpse of hardship, becoming hopeless and losing courage, while others have the drive to fight on. As God's people, we must stand on Scripture—the Bible—in the midst of adversity and lean on His strong arm because we ARE coming out of our trials!

Tips to Developing Your Spiritual Perception

1) Be open to hear from God—even things you would rather not.

If you are open to allow the Lord to give you direction and guidance without allowing your personal feelings to color your predicament, it can be life-changing. Many are not reachable though, but walled off, because of preconceived thoughts and ideas, even religious beliefs that are not founded on scriptural principles. So be available to obtain a fresh biblical directive from the Lord.

> "'For I know the plans I have for you,' says the Lord. 'They are plans for good and not for disaster, to give you a future and a hope'" (Jeremiah 29:11, NLT).

God's plan isn't a disastrous plan, but one that gives you a future to look forward to and gives hope to turn things for the better. God has a good plan, and you will be pleased with it. You do not have to fear or resist. We are to make ourselves available to discern God's voice. I did not understand that He speaks to believers until I began to read the Bible for myself and realized this was possible.

> "I am the Good Shepherd and know my own sheep, and they know me...My sheep recognize My voice, and I know them, and they follow Me" (John 10:14, 27, TLB).

Don't make up your mind about something without first considering what the Lord has for you. There are times we run past wisdom and what's best for us. We can be headstrong or stubborn and have to find out the hard way that His way was the way to victory, and our way was not. I have found in many years of pastoring that there are those who want to be in public ministry so badly they can run over God's purpose for their lives in pursuit of their own plan.We are told in Scripture that the rebellious dwell in a dry place (Psalm 68:6). In a dry place, there's no growth or flourishing, and that's not a place to be.

"For rebellion is as the sin of witchcraft, and stubbornness is as iniquity and idolatry" (1 Samuel 15:23).

There should be no rebellion in us, but rather an obedient, pliant spirit. Right?

2) God Speaks through the Bible.

Jesus is the Word made into flesh (John 1:14). That's an astounding statement. When you read the Bible, you are partaking of Jesus—His character, abilities, attitudes, and all that He is. There is miraculous power found in the Scripture, and you can release it into your life and apply it to your "mountain of human obstacles."

"Sanctify them through thy truth: thy word is truth" (John 17:17).

We live in a time when people in our society believe there is no absolute truth—no right or wrong—nothing moral or immoral. However, this is incorrect, and that's why society is in such chaos. If you're seeking to hear God's direction as you read the

Bible, be open for Him to quicken truth to you to affirm or confirm His plan. His Word is absolute truth. You are sanctified or set apart for God's purpose through His truth.

3) Create an atmosphere of peace.

> "And after the earthquake a fire; but the Lord was not in the fire: and after the fire a still small voice" (1 Kings 19:12).

Sometimes life is so frantic, cluttered, and hectic there is no way to receive divine comfort and peace from God. However, as you still yourself quietly before the Lord, He can amaze you by dropping into your heart specific wisdom and direction for what you're facing. I regularly sit quietly in God's presence and ask Him to impart to me what I need—be it peace, calm, correction. I do not ask anything at that time; I simply receive from Him. It's remarkable how this brings tranquility into my soul and helps me to deal with what's at hand.

4) Don't rely on emotions or feelings.

> "But none of these things move me" (Acts 20:24).

Feelings can be very misleading and get you sidetracked and way off course. Your emotions can change from one moment to the next. However, we are to be steady, having a firm foundation in Scripture and not in the emotional fluctuations of life. If you depend on your senses, you can be misled. Place faith in what God says—it is unchanging—trust Him and then dig your spiritual heels against the enemy until you receive your promise. Tell yourself and the enemy of your soul what the Bible says. Stand securely on that; don't be moved by the way things appear or how you feel!

5) Wait to see if the witness of the Holy Spirit becomes stronger.

> "Howbeit when he, the Spirit of truth, is come, he will guide you into all truth" (John 16:13).

When you sense you are hearing from the Holy Spirit, do not quickly or hastily move out into something. Wait to see if the impression continues and grows stronger. Being assured that you know what you're doing will instill confidence in you. Going slowly may save you much trouble and is a particularly significant component in being led by the Spirit. Of course, as the leading persists, move forward; there's no value in procrastinating after you believe you are following the Lord's guidance.

Recharging When Life Wears You Down

CHAPTER 9

ABOUT RECHARGING

This chapter defines the need to find freshness and newness in your walk with the Lord when difficult times have worn you down and stripped you of your zeal and enthusiasm. It is a step to assist you in the progression from being fainthearted to bursting with God's presence—not just functioning, but conquering the circumstances that have knocked you down. While you're reading this, you may feel weary and depleted, so I'm sharing this information to help you.

> "We get knocked down, but we get up again and keep going" (2 Corinthians 4:9, TLB).

All of us can be knocked down by life's circumstances, but we don't have to stay down. This chapter hopefully will help you find your way and encourage you to get up and keep going despite things you are going through.

I have some beautiful candles in my home. I set candles on my mantle and around the house, and they create a warm and inviting atmosphere. They look like real candles at a distance, but they are battery operated. Every so often, the batteries lose their power and have to be replaced. After the candles have been glowing for a month or two, new batteries need to be installed. In our lives, when our "spiritual batteries" become weak, our light begins to wane, and we must take action for ourselves. The Lord knows the challenges of life can wear us down, but you can do certain things to "power up" your life.

Here's something that may have happened to you. You are rushing around in the morning, getting ready for work. You pile all your incredibly important stuff in the back seat, plop down behind the wheel, turn the key, and bzzzzzz—the car won't start. The battery is dead; the car won't move. It isn't functioning the way it should. In our lives, that's the way it is for us at times. We are drained. Life—the cares of life and overwhelming circumstances—can empty us, and we find ourselves in need of spiritual power or recharging to move forward when we don't seem to be able.

At one time, you can be on fire for God, but later, you can be lethargic and apathetic, spiritually sapped, and feeling used up. Sometimes we don't have the spiritual vitality that we need. I understand the lack of physical energy and poor health will absolutely interfere with your spiritual life, but I'm referring to spiritual energy needing to be replenished. There are times when we all need to be recharged. To recharge means to refresh or restore, to revitalize, to revive or restore energy.

A similar word used in Scripture is "edify," which means to charge like a battery. When a car battery is dead, it has to be recharged to possess the energy to function properly. It also means to build up like a house. The building process for a house begins by laying a foundation, which becomes the place where everything else concerning the building process rests.

When you're unenthusiastic and don't have the zeal that you once had for the Lord, then it's time for you to take action. It's time to decide to see this reversed by doing things God's way. The problems and difficulties we experience in life can drain us of our spiritual energy, but enthusiasm for God is crucial, and you can take steps to change your situation.

Maintaining Enthusiasm for God

Many have matured in their faith and have experienced growth in God. I can identify with that, but I don't equate "mature" with being spiritually dead and dry. It is possible to walk with the Lord for a long time and still maintain your fervor for Him. Enthusiasm is a derivative of the word that means "God in us." So, if God is in you, you should be enthusiastic. Right? Well, hopefully!

Recharging also has to do with stamina. When you're spiritually energized, you have something that keeps you going when others aren't able and are placed on the sidelines. I am talking about recharging by the power of Holy Spirit.

Scripture has many examples of those who had setbacks that diminished their spiritual power, but then they were able to bounce back. The Lord wants to refresh us and renew our spiritual vitality. Then joy and enthusiasm can be restored to us again. So, it's possible to regain momentum and "recharge" your spiritual life, no matter what your mind or the enemy is speaking to you.

CHAPTER 10

WAYS TO RECHARGE

Ask God for Help

The **first** way to recharge is simply to ASK God to help you. Asking God for His assistance in our lives is His very own idea!

"Yet you do not have, because you do no ask"
(James 4:2, NKJV).

"Jesus said, 'I am the vine and you are the branches'"
(John 15:5).

Branches draw their strength, their supply, and everything they need from the vine. So we're not talking about self-sufficiency. Many times we think and talk about our problem, but never take the step of asking God to help us in our depleted condition.

Prayer—asking God—is a lifeline. Many people talk a lot about prayer, but don't ever actually do that much praying! If you take time to sit down in the presence of the Lord, He will give ability, insight, and help to overcome the things that you are dealing with in life. It is amazing what spending time in the Lord's presence will do for a Christian. When we experience a lack of zeal for God or even a lack of spiritual energy, we can call upon our great and mighty God, and He will begin to fill our spiritual tanks.

> Call to Me and I will answer you and show you great and mighty things, fenced in and hidden, which you do not know (do not distinguish and recognize, have knowledge of and understand) (Jeremiah 33:3, AMPC).

"Ask me and I will tell you remarkable secrets you do not know about things to come" (Jeremiah 33:3, NLT).

God says He will answer us and reveal amazing privileged information that He has hidden—now listen to this—**for** us, not **from** us. Spending time in the Father's presence is vital. He can unfold secrets to us about ourselves, loved ones, and our situation. The world's wisdom and knowledge have no way to take us into the depths of these fascinating secrets and mysteries of God. We cannot receive this enlightenment if we don't steal away and draw from Christ, the Vine. Expect that when He declares and brings revelation, it will bring light and help to change your situation. Through this revelation, you can be encouraged and strengthened. Then you will find your zeal for God returning.

If you have a lot of drama in your life and you draw aside with the Lord, you may hear Him say, "I want you to apologize for that nasty attitude you had with your spouse," or "I want you to tell your children that you were wrong in losing your temper when you disciplined them." In dealing with issues, you remove blockages that stop you from hearing and receiving from the

Lord. It will lead you on the path to recharging because these things can hinder and erode your spiritual power. God has the answers. The things that stand in your way can be overcome as He opens your eyes to see things that have been obscured.

In pastoring, I see people who are on fire for God. They're sharing their faith; they're living a life that exemplifies Christ. The next thing you know, they've lost their zeal; they're worn down, offended, and possibly mad or bitter at God. Afterward, they become angry with people, and their walk with God becomes distant. Consequently, they are living a life of defeat. So, you must be proactive concerning your spiritual life and do something to fight back against spiritual apathy.

Read the Bible

The **second** way to recharge is to begin to read the Bible daily. If you're not a person who reads the Bible, you might start with reading one chapter each day. Baby steps are important here. It will begin to nourish your spirit man. I'm talking about when you begin the recharging process because you've probably let your Bible and prayer habits decline. But when I say you should read a chapter a day, I'm talking about only until you establish better spiritual habits. Afterward, I recommend that you read more than a chapter a day to advance and grow in God.

> My son, attend to my words; incline thine ear unto my sayings. Let them not depart from thine eyes; keep them in the midst of thine heart. For they are life unto those that find them, and health to all their flesh (Proverbs 4:20).

This verse advises us to look after or pay attention to what's written in Scripture and not allow it to slip from your thinking. We are told to give our ear to His sayings, which means to stretch, turn, or yield to the truths you're seeing. Other voices may be vying for your attention, but turn away from them and stretch forward toward the Lord yielding to His Word.

Scripture consistently needs to be before your eyes and in your mind to renew your thoughts, updating the way you think about life and other things. It also must be in your heart because the heart is where God speaks. It's where direction comes into your life from the Lord, telling you how to live and which way you need to go.

The word "life" in the Greek is *zoë*—God's life—the life of God dwells in YOU. When you read your Bible, you are receiving this *zoë* life. Scripture says the Word of God is medicine to our flesh (Proverbs 4:22). Taken as directed and applied, it will cure our problems and the issues of life! Jesus is the Great Physician and can heal your ills—all of them!

Just recently for our wedding anniversary, we decided we weren't going to a restaurant, but we would stay home and prepare a delicious meal. Before we began eating, I was absolutely starving. Everything smelled and looked delicious to me. Sometimes that's the way I feel about the Word of God. I cannot wait to open the pages and dig into it because I know God is going to speak to me, reveal something to me, talk to me, and impart to me truths that will bring great freedom in my life. I am hungry to be with Him. So when we're talking about recharging, we have to remember that we must get in the Bible and allow the Bible to get into us! You may start small by reading a chapter a day, but then you will experience an increased appetite and desire for God's Word!

When I first was filled with the Holy Spirit, I experienced a new and great appetite for the Word of God. No joke, when I would read the Bible, everything I read seemed to jump off the page and spoke directly to me. I began to see magnificent, life-changing truths. It radically changed my life and established my pathway to God's plan. When you read your Bible, you may be like me and underline things that speak to you. Well, I have underlined almost everything in my Bible because God was imparting Himself to me through this life-changing book! It resonated and brought direction, purpose, guidelines, and boundaries into my life. Do you want to have a good marriage? Find out what the Bible says about marriage and practice it. Do you want to relate better to others? Then find out what the Bible says about relationships. Do you want to be a good church member? Then find out what the Bible says about that and apply it. Do you want to be enthusiastic about God? Well, you're finding out here different ways to stir yourself and receive—just apply it.

I enjoy reading Psalms and Proverbs, so I add it to my daily reading. When in Proverbs, whatever the date is, that's the proverb I read. Reading Psalms is a great way to keep your heart right before God. Psalms gives you examples of worship and praise, and it shares the struggles the writers experienced. These will nourish you and keep you tender and sensitive to the Lord.

Scriptural preaching and teaching of the Bible will also charge you up spiritually. I like to listen to messages in my car of someone preaching the Word of God to me. I listen to faith-inspiring preaching most of the time. I'll listen to other subjects—I don't want to be short-sighted in my walk with the Lord—but so many times, I need faith-filled teaching because of the things I face daily. I need information and inspiration which will produce transformation! Doing this helps me in no small way to deal with life and its many challenges. The teachings tell me things that encourage and impart faith and hope. You cannot read every moment of the day, but you can get somebody preaching and teaching to you at various times when you cannot read yourself. I find ministers who feed my spirit, such as Reverend Aquila Nash with the Prophetic Whisper television program, so when I'm getting ready for work, I listen to her inspiring messages. She always teaches motivating truths at the right time for me to hear. It encourages me and keeps the Word of God "before my eyes," as described in Proverbs. This process emboldens me to be a better person and helps keep God's fire in my life. It will do the same for you.

Being Filled with the Holy Spirit

The **third** way to recharge is to be filled or refilled with the Holy Spirit. After our salvation, there is a separate experience—being filled with the Holy Spirit (Acts and Ephesians reveal this). At the time we are saved, we, of course, receive God's Spirit, but being filled or baptized with the Holy Spirit is another step that takes you deeper in your relationship with God as revealed in Scripture. When you are filled with the Holy Spirit, you receive your personal prayer language, and your life is opened to the things of the Spirit. This simple explanation is only to introduce you to a profound and dynamic truth that is available to you that I cover in depth in chapter 11.

> "And be not drunk with wine, wherein is excess; but be filled with the Spirit" (Ephesians 5:18).

This verse is emphasizing that we are to continue being filled with the Spirit. The Amplified Bible says, "...but ever be filled and stimulated with the [Holy] Spirit." There's not just an initial infilling, and that's all there is to it! It's a continual refilling of the Holy Spirit. Why? We are continually facing situations in life that deplete us, or we are ministering to others that can take away from our spiritual energy. Because of this, we need to be filled continuously! What happened to you 50 years ago is great, but what's happening in you today?

It's really interesting to me that the words "don't be drunk with wine" appear in Ephesians, chapter five. When people drink too much, they get filled with alcohol. They believe they're having fun, but they are intoxicated, not thinking clearly or talking sensibly. Sometimes, foolish things are done, which are unthinkable under normal circumstances and detrimental. The Bible clearly states that we are not to be intoxicated with wine where we act foolishly, but be intoxicated with God's Spirit—be filled up to overflowing. So, we can readily see that we need to continuously be filled with the Spirit, which is an ongoing process. You will live differently, act differently, and talk differently—never foolishly.

We will see that this third way to recharge is strongly associated with the seventh way to recharge that we will discuss later on.

Staying Full of God's Presence

> "Speaking to yourselves in psalms and hymns and spiritual songs, singing and making melody in your heart to the Lord" (Ephesians 5:19).

The **fourth** way to recharge is to stay full of God's presence. This verse is really fascinating to me. You sing and make melody in your heart to the Lord, and it doesn't matter if you sound great or not! What does matter is that you're singing from your heart to the Lord using psalms, hymns, and spiritual songs to worship Him. These precipitate staying full of the Holy Spirit. This process is spiritually received, and not received through your human reasoning. Sometimes I will hear a song that is uplifting to me, and I'll sing it all week! I'm recharging! God has spoken to me before and said, "You've lost your song!" And I knew exactly what He meant: I was not in the place I needed to be—full of God's Spirit—and I needed to change and press into this scriptural truth. As you sing, you'll also find your joy will return.

The book of Psalms is useful to help you move into God's presence. At times, the Holy Spirit may give you your own psalm; you should be sure to use this special and unique psalm to worship the Lord. When I first received the infilling of the Holy Spirit and learned these things I am sharing, I would be reading in the book of Psalms, and suddenly God would give me a tune to go with a Psalm. I have these personal psalms recorded so I won't lose them. I didn't know much back then about what I am telling you now. No one taught this to me. The songs came up out of my spirit and would bubble up in me as I read the Psalms.

In our church, we don't have hymnals, but I was raised in a church that used them. A lot of the hymns we sang were really good songs: "The Old Rugged Cross," "At the Cross," "Victory in Jesus," "Power in the Blood," "Just as I Am." Think about those songs; they are timeless hymns. When I remember "Just as I Am," I think about Reverend Billy Graham's crusades. I rededicated my life to the Lord when he was in Knoxville, Tennessee in 1970. This, of course, was a very defining moment that changed my life and spiritual direction. He and this song are very special to me. I've never tired of hearing this old hymn. Hymns are full of biblical truths, and as you sing them, scriptural principles are reinforced, which causes faith to rise and increase. Many songs today can be far from scriptural and are not the songs to which I'm referring.

So, psalms, hymns, and spiritual songs are inspired songs, and they can be used when something difficult is going on in your life. Spiritual songs, hymns, and psalms are important and should be taken with you into your prayer closet. They are key elements in helping you to recharge.

Spiritual songs represent what's occurring in your life now and singing forth principles found in Scripture that provide answers, recharges you, and gives you victory. When the children of Israel were crossing the Red Sea and came to the other side, the women had their tambourines in hand and began singing about the horse and the rider thrown into the sea as the enemy chased after God's people. Maybe you need to start singing about the "horse and the rider thrown into the sea" in your life and how you're going to get to the other side. Rejoice!

Praising God

The **fifth** way to recharge is to praise God. In Psalm 150, there are six things that God tells us about praising Him:

> Praise ye the Lord. Praise God in his sanctuary: praise him in the firmament of his power. Praise him for his mighty acts: praise him according to his excellent greatness. Praise him with the sound of the trumpet: praise him with the psaltery and harp. Praise him with the timbrel and dance: praise him with stringed instruments and organs. Praise him upon the loud cymbals: praise him upon the high sounding cymbals. Let every thing that hath breath praise the Lord. Praise ye the Lord (Psalm 150).

1) We're to praise Him in our corporate services. Don't be embarrassed to praise the Lord, to lift your hands, and to sing and rejoice in the Lord. There is no need to be ashamed—push pride aside.
2) Both saints on earth and angels in heaven are to praise Him.
3) Praise Him in the firmament. (This earth!)
4) Praise Him for what He's done and for who He is.
5) Praise Him with instruments.
6) Praise Him with the dance. There's a kind of dance that doesn't bring glory to God, but there is a dance that we can be involved in that does bring glory to God.

Waiting

> He giveth power to the faint; and to them that have no might he increaseth strength. Even the youths shall faint and be weary, and the young men shall utterly fall: But they that wait upon the Lord shall renew their strength; they shall mount up with wings as eagles; they shall run,

> and not be weary; and they shall walk, and not
> faint (Isaiah 40:29-31).

We think of the young as full of strength and stamina and that they won't stumble, but He said even the young men can get fatigued and falter. It doesn't matter how old or young you are.

The **sixth** way to recharge is to wait on the Lord. To wait on the Lord means to minister and serve as a server in a restaurant would attend to patrons. We are reminded in this verse that those who "wait" on the Lord—spend time in God's presence worshipping Him—shall renew their strength by exchanging their weakness to accelerate in His strength. Then we're told we will run, but not grow weary. This verse is a wonderful promise. We are told that in His presence is fullness of joy. If we've lost our joy, we may not be spending enough time waiting on the Lord and being still.

Praying in Tongues

The **seventh** way to jumpstart the recharging process is to pray in the Spirit—pray in tongues. You receive your prayer language after you are filled with the Holy Spirit. When you need to be recharged, and you're weary and worn down, using your prayer language is key to refreshing yourself.

When you've lost the edge in prayer, begin praying in tongues a few minutes every day. Then increase the time and keep increasing it until you get your prayer time with the Lord on target.

I didn't understand the great power and benefit of praying in tongues at first. I was brought up in a denomination where they didn't know about or practice being filled with the Spirit and speaking in a heavenly language. My church loved God and told me how to be born again, and for that, I'm very thankful. My dad was the pastor of the church I grew up in, and he had some remarkable revelations of God's Word, but he didn't understand the baptism of the Holy Spirit. So, when I started reading this truth in the Bible and saw it for the first time, it was foreign to me. We tend to discount something when it is unknown to us, or we might look over it. We might say, "That's not for me. That's good for you, but not for me." God is no respecter of persons, and He didn't give this promise for one person or one group. He wrote this truth for all believers to see, understand, and receive. If one person needs the equipping of being filled with the Holy Spirit and speaking with other tongues, we all do. We all may not receive it, but we cannot say it's not for us—whosoever will may come!

> "And they were all filled with the Holy Spirit, and began to speak with other tongues, as the Spirit gave them utterance" (Acts 2:4, NKJV).

The initial evidence of being filled with the Spirit is speaking in other tongues (see Chapter 11), and your ongoing personal prayer language makes a world of difference in your spiritual growth. Jesus Christ is the same yesterday, today, and forever (Hebrews 13:8). What we see in the Bible, He's still doing today.

It took me a while to fully grasp the truth of the infilling of the Holy Spirit. For people who attend our church now, it isn't a lengthy discovery process because we biblically teach them and lead them into it. My husband and I read it for ourselves and discovered it without a teacher or spiritual guide. When God called us to pastor, we began to share these marvelous truths with those to whom we ministered, and many received. Today, we are still teaching this relevant truth of the Holy Spirit consistently and making it clear for those who want to receive. Praying in tongues is very important in the charging up process!

CHAPTER 11

THE HOLY SPIRIT

In this chapter, I want to share a scriptural experience about which you may or may not be familiar, but it will radically change your life. I'm providing a simplistic overview of a profound truth about the infilling of the Holy Spirit; you can find many comprehensive books on this topic. I believe if you lay hold of this truth, like many Christians around the world, it will bring dynamic power to your life that will take your relationship with the Lord to a different level and chart the course for your future.

Infilling

Being filled with the Holy Spirit, also known as the baptism of the Spirit or the infilling, is a New Testament practice found in many denominations and encountered today by millions of people. It is an authentic Christian experience, whether you may have heard of it before or not. This fascinating scriptural occurrence will empower you daily and will tremendously aid you during a challenging time.

The Bible says that when you receive the infilling of the Holy Spirit, you have God's presence working in you to be a witness of His power and love. Before I received the infilling, I simply had no power to influence others for the Lord and quite possibly took people in the other direction! I accepted Jesus as my Lord but didn't have stability in my walk with God. However, when I read the Bible in its entirety, these truths brought a spiritual inquisitiveness that made me want what God had for me, and I set out to discover more.

"But you shall receive power when the Holy Spirit has come upon you; and you shall be witnesses to Me in Jerusalem, and in all Judea and Samaria, and to the end of the earth" (Acts 1:8, NKJV).

Let me make this clear: when you come to God and accept Jesus Christ as your Savior and Lord, you receive God's Spirit; I certainly am not detracting from the salvation experience. Romans 8:9 says, "But ye are not in the flesh, but in the Spirit, if so be that the Spirit of God dwell in you. Now if any man have not the Spirit of Christ, he is none of his."

As you read further into the New Testament, you see the infilling of the Holy Spirit is a separate experience from salvation that endows the believer with a dynamic equipping. I found myself to be hungry and thirsty to discover more about the Father, Son, and Holy Spirit! I began to see things I had never realized, even though I was raised in a Bible-believing home. It was a captivating time in my life that continues even today. How do you activate this truth in your life?

> If a son shall ask bread of any of you that is a father, will he give him a stone? or if he ask a fish, will he for a fish give him a serpent? Or if he shall ask an egg, will he offer him a scorpion? If ye then, being evil, know how to give good gifts unto your children: how much

> more shall your heavenly Father give the Holy Spirit to them that **ask** him? (Luke 11:11, emphasis added).

This verse indicates that to receive this significant experience, we must ASK God for the Holy Spirit's infilling. We need not fear a counterfeit encounter. When we ask God, He will meet us without interference from any other realm.

Here is a list of Bible references that you can read for yourself to bring insight into this incredible adventure in God:

- Joel 2:28-29 (the outpouring)
- Acts 2:39 (the promise)
- Acts 1:5 (the baptism of the Holy Spirit)
- Acts 19:2 (born-again believers receiving)
- Acts 10:9, 10, 13 (for believers in Christ Jesus only)
- Acts 2:4 (the sign of spiritual language)
- 1 Corinthians 14:2 (communication with God)
- 1 Corinthians 14:4 (strengthens you)

Spiritual Language

"For he that speaketh in an unknown tongue speaketh not unto men, but unto God: for no man understandeth him; howbeit in the spirit he speaketh mysteries" (1 Corinthians 14:2).

The Bible says your connection with the Holy Spirit gives you an ability to receive a supernatural language that you did not learn or study that will "charge" your spirit, like a battery. Receiving this supernatural language is evidence of the infilling of the Holy Spirit. Some may not fully understand this truth, but we want to be on target scripturally and believe and practice the Word of God—not follow religious training that has no biblical precedent. How do you speak in an unknown language? This is a supernatural happening, but don't shy away from it. You don't study for it; you receive the infilling by faith.

I refuse to live without the power of the Holy Spirit in my life and without the ability to pray in tongues. Some think this is foolish, emotional, and unnecessary, but that is so far from the truth. This experience is totally biblical and equips you to speak to the Lord, and it provides a way for Him to speak remarkable "secrets" and divine mysteries directly to you. It goes far beyond our intellectual prayers, as powerful as they are!

Scripture teaches us that when you pray in tongues, you edify, build up, and enhance your life: "He who speaks in a tongue edifies himself" (1 Corinthians 14:4, NKJV). You can use your private devotional prayer language and recharge yourself spiritually, which will affect your whole person—spirit, soul, and even body. As we live life, we can be depleted of spiritual power, but praying in the Spirit is a way to solve this problem and be entirely filled with God's presence!

Jude 1:20 says, "But you, beloved, building yourselves up on your most holy faith, praying in the Holy Spirit." This verse teaches us that when you pray in your spiritual language, it fortifies you and helps you to stand firm. It instills God's strength in you and assists you in overcoming weaknesses.

> Likewise, the Spirit also helps in our weaknesses. For we do not know what we should pray for as we ought, but the Spirit Himself makes intercession for us with groanings which cannot be uttered. Now He who searches the hearts

> knows what the mind of the Spirit is, because He makes intercession for the saints according to the will of God (Romans 8:26-27).

These verses show that when we pray in the Spirit, we are speaking directly to God and praying His perfect will. This truth is awesome! There's no way we could pray perfectly with our own intellect; we don't have the ability on our own to pray a perfect prayer. However, the Lord gives us this capability to tap into His wisdom and knowledge, and it is His great, all-knowing, all-seeing discernment that equips us to pray in this way.

Praying in our spiritual language is two-pronged: personal and public. When I talk about speaking in tongues here, I am referencing the personal, devotional use of tongues. The public gifts of the Holy Spirit are available to Christians once they are filled with the Spirit (1 Corinthians 12), which includes the spiritual gift of tongues with interpretation. These public gifts did not pass away, as some have said; the Holy Spirit is still in operation today! Familiarize yourself with these public gifts, but what I am referring to here is your own private devotional language that allows you to converse with your Creator.

Praying in tongues allows you to pray for yourself and others. When I don't know what to pray, I'll pray in English first, but I have limited knowledge about the situation. Then I pray in the spirit with the Holy Spirit taking hold together with me to pray God's will. That's powerful! Who wouldn't want this ability? When I don't know how to pray, the Holy Spirit prays through me exactly what needs to be said. As I pray in other tongues and yield myself, God uses me to pray forth the answer. This requires faith to move in and trust His Word on the subject. Praying in the Spirit adds great dimension and definition to our prayer life and is another remarkable and compelling weapon in God's arsenal offered to His family.

"For with stammering lips and another tongue will he speak to this people. To whom he said, This is the rest wherewith ye may cause the weary to rest; and this is the refreshing: yet they would not hear" (Isaiah 28:11-12).

This prophetic passage looks forward to New Testament believers having a way for God to communicate directly with us. God gives us a prayer language to tap into His supernatural power, but some refuse to believe and heed. Not me! I desire to hear more clearly and effectively.

Circumstances in life can make you bitter and hard. I've known people that have been through much pain and hardship, and it showed on their countenance. But when a believer prays in the spirit, their countenance transforms as their hearts become sensitive and softened. When your heart is calloused with cares, difficulties, and/or strife, it is challenging for your spirit to receive from the Lord, but you can help turn that around by praying with your spiritual language.

When I pray in the spirit, I do so in faith. God doesn't give me insight every time I pray, but I continue with confidence, knowing that praying in tongues edifies and builds up my spirit, and refreshes me. I may not understand everything, but if it's the Lord, I want to press in to know more.

Spiritual Attacks

CHAPTER 12

INDICATORS OF A SPIRITUAL ATTACK

When troublesome times surround you, it is essential to understand that spiritual attacks are real. When you have understanding , you can deal with them effectively. You may be under attack whether you are oblivious to it or not; it is still real and destructive.

You may not be experiencing a spiritual attack at this time, but everyone has been through them, even though it may not have been discerned or acknowledged. Realizing how to recognize and handle these assaults is extremely vital. Your strategy should be formulated using Scripture to combat and defeat the assault. The Bible is the guidebook on how to resist in a time of spiritual onslaught and gain victory over it.

When we talk about spiritual attacks, the first step of action is to believe that the devil and demon powers are real. I read a statistic saying that among proclaiming Christians, over 60% do not believe the devil exists. Isn't that just like the enemy to blind and disarm people to the truth? Because they're uninformed and don't recognize what's happening, he enters or encroaches into their lives, and they're unable to discern what's happening to them.

On the other hand, some people talk much about satan and emphasize his work—the devil this and the devil that. When I hear this, it tells me that they're glorifying the devil rather than glorifying God. I heard this story about a country church where the people would give testimonies in services. One woman stood up and said, "The devil's been working against me all week. Bless his holy name." She, of course, meant to bless the name of the Lord, but that's not what she said or was doing! She was unknowingly glorifying the devil instead of the Lord. Yes, the devil may be charging against you, but you always triumph in Christ Jesus. Choose to give the Lord recognition for His defeat of satan at Calvary.

In the Scripture, you'll see that Jesus talked much about spiritual assaults from the enemy and how to deal with him. That's very different from today. The epistles are also especially revealing. When there is a large section of believers who do not believe the devil is real, the enemy has them right where he wants them. He attacks and then tells them that God did it! Because of this, people live oppressed lives, believing there's nothing they can do about their predicament, but endure. The enemy even tells people that the attack glorifies God! No! We are to stand our ground and resist his lies and his intrusion.

> "Submit yourselves therefore to God. RESIST THE DEVIL, AND HE WILL FLEE FROM YOU" (James 4:7, emphasis added).

Many of the things that happen in our lives aren't coincidences but are well-conceived plans and strategies that are laid out by an evil force. Once we have submitted to the Lord, we can successfully resist or contend against evil works and not lie down to be overthrown. There's an enemy against the work of

God and the lives of His people. Paul talked about a large door of opportunity given to him—but "there are many adversaries" (1 Corinthians 6:9). If Paul had adversaries, we who are believers also have adversaries. These enemies can be people, of course, but they can also be invisible enemies. I do have good news! While there are many adversaries, there are many angelic beings who are given to help us in overcoming our opponents' destructive plots. These angelic beings aid us, but did you know that the angels do not respond until we speak a specific way?

> "Bless the Lord, ye his angels, that excel in strength, that do his commandments, **hearkening unto the voice of his word**" (Psalm 103:20, emphasis added).

Angels, the Bible says, listen for you to speak and release Scriptures over your situation. When you speak the Word of God, it gives angels permission to intervene on your behalf. He has placed principles in the kingdom, and when we agree and speak those truths, angels are commissioned to go to work on our behalf. There is tremendous power in the Word of God to bring His promises to pass. In difficult situations, fight back by arming yourself against these spiritual attacks.

Battle by Using Scriptures

I carry my Bible with me everywhere I go. I have my Bible reading app on my phone, and I love to read it. Scripture is precious to me. It's the Holy Word of God, not because of the leather and the paper—it's the power of God that's on each page. When we read the Bible, we take it into our hearts and minds to update our thinking. Then we are enabled by the faith it brings to believe it and speak it. It will penetrate and cause us to change. Then things around us begin to change.

We are to glorify God in the midst of a spiritual attack and thank Him for rescuing us. (We are not thanking Him FOR the attack!) I want to present God's Word to you on this subject and come to a well-balanced place. A ministry friend of mine said she knew a Spirit-filled man, and he told her that he never talks about the devil. Well, I understand that if it's to an extreme, as in too much emphasis on the devil, but he was saying, "I'm not going to recognize him, so that he won't bother me." My friend said, "Well, I've got news for you. That won't stop him. He will work in your life regardless and probably accomplish much more." So just because we don't acknowledge the enemy doesn't mean that he's not working against us or attacking our lives.

> Be sober [well balanced and self-disciplined], be alert and cautious at all times. That enemy of yours, the devil, prowls around like a roaring lion [fiercely hungry], seeking someone to devour (1 Peter 5:8, AMP).

For the Christian, our balance must come from the Word of God without sprinkling in religious traditions that have been passed down to us. If it doesn't line up scripturally, it's only a tradition of man, not the divinely inspired Word of God. In my earlier years, I heard some religious traditions mixed with Scripture. Then, as I started reading the Bible for myself, I realized some things were not in the Bible or were taken out of context. We need to be like the Berean believers: search the Word to discover the truths for ourselves. The Word of God being preached by someone is powerful, but it is also powerful when you read it, speak it, and act upon it yourself. It's miraculous! It will never fail you. Circumstances and people can let you down, but God's Word will never disappoint you.

Notice in First Peter 5:8, the devil is seeking someone to devour which indicates he is unable to succeed in attacking all. Those who are alert and paying attention to him are the ones who win. Be alert and resist him!

At times, there can be long-standing attacks working against us. Here is an example of this in my own life. We had sold our home and moved from Knoxville to California for my husband to go to seminary. Then later, God impressed us to come back to Knoxville to start a new church. We didn't have a place to live, so we leased a home that was admittedly less than desirable. But we did our best to fix it up and make it as nice as we could. We started the church, and it was financial fight of faith. Things began to happen to our appliances, one after the other. Our clothes dryer stopped working, so I called a repairman. But, he couldn't find anything wrong with the dryer. After that, our washer also stopped working. Then, my dishwasher wouldn't work. My dishwasher was the last straw! With a new church and limited personal finances, there wasn't enough money to replace or repair all those appliances. It dawned on me one day that we were under spiritual attack for following the Lord! We had begun this new work for the God, and the enemy wanted to discourage, distract, and pull us away from the purpose of God.

Ed, my husband, was in his study for what seemed like 24 hours-a-day. He was fast and furious in the Word, learning and growing. I went to him about this, and he told me, "You need to handle it! I'm busy." So, I did. I bound the spirit of destruction off our possessions.

When you're taking steps of faith to follow God, you must stand your ground! In our case, God assigned us a city in the

Bible Belt that had a lot of religious traditions to combat, but we were dedicated to proclaim His truth and stand firm.

I said to myself, "I'm going to resist this attack, in Jesus' name." So, I laid my hands on the washer, and I said, "You are going to work! I command you to work, in the name of Jesus." I went to my dryer, and I said, "You are going to dry my clothes, and you are going to work." And I laid my hands on the dishwasher, and I said, "You wash my dishes. You're going to obey, in Jesus' name." Do you think it didn't work, and I was greatly disappointed? No, it worked! I washed and dried clothes and cleaned my dishes for the whole time I lived in that place with those same appliances. And when I moved out of that house, I gave those appliances to someone else—and I didn't give them in disrepair! As you can see, those appliances weren't old and used up; we were under attack.

I realize that you must be balanced here. When something is worn out and used up, I surely replace it. I'm not trying to be ridiculous, but rather to show how to make a stand of faith in challenging times when you are under an onslaught. I did not collapse in a chair and cry, "Oh my God, we're doing what you told us to do. What do you expect from us?" Would that have produced results? No, it would not. When the spiritual barrage comes, we must deal with it God's way, and that is not by whining or complaining.

"And the seventy returned again with joy, saying,
Lord, even the devils are subject unto us through thy name"
(Luke 10:17).

The truths that I'm sharing with you, I've learned through everyday living and applying these biblical truths through faith.

God wants to strip the cover off works of darkness and reveal things to us, so then we can successfully deal with them by using the powerful name of Jesus.

Recognize What's Going On

Years ago, I read an article that shared similar things to what I'm sharing here, and it inspired me to meditate on it and develop the following points to help recognize a spiritual attack.

1) Spiritual Confusion

The first sign that you're under attack is when there is confusion concerning spiritual direction. Confusion is sent to rob you of your future in God. I couldn't even enumerate how many times I've seen this while pastoring. Individuals in the congregation can be growing and flourishing spiritually—lives changed—then from out of nowhere, a friend says something about their church—even though their friend has never attended. The person then takes on a secondhand offense and decides they are moving to another fellowship. Do you understand that your spiritual destiny is connected to the church where God has placed you? If a church is Christ-centered and biblically based, God wants use that local fellowship in your life. When people begin to speak things against the place where your spiritual growth is found and centered, it could rob you of your God-given destiny by discouraging you and pulling you off track if you listen to it.

Does God ever move people to a different fellowship? Of course, He does, but I believe God sets the solitary in a spiritual family (Psalm 68:6). We're not to be "cruiseamatics" that just run from one church to another. We need to find the place where we belong, settle down, and get involved and connected by working our way through any adjustment period. Sometimes we may be in the place and time of stretching and growing in Christ. If you have not found your church home, then keep searching until the Holy Spirit reveals it to you. If you know that you're in the right place, stay connected, settle in, and don't allow the enemy, by using others, to change your direction. There is no perfect fellowship because they are all full of imperfect people just like us! Some people stop attending church, and then they become halfhearted in their relationship with the Lord. The next thing you know, they are having marriage problems, financial problems, and on and on. I do understand you can experience those things even when you're close to the Lord, but you will come out of it victoriously if you stand steady on the promises of God.

2) The Urge to Quit

The **second** sign to consider when you're under spiritual attack is a strong urge to quit your assignment. You start thinking, "Nobody appreciates me, so I'm not going to continue to do this." I am preaching to myself here; I've had to live out some of what I'm sharing with you. Therefore, I want to emphasize it! What is this about—this discouragement to quit? It's to get you sidetracked. You have a unique purpose with uncommon grace, and you have been given the gifts and equipping to fulfill what God wants for your life. Not everybody is called to be in public ministry, so I'm not just talking about that. Your assignment may be a business person, or in some way serve humanity through your calling (doctor, nurse, etc.), or to focus on investing in your family by being a dedicated mother or father. Whatever the calling, we need to put our hearts into our assignment and have no quitting sense, if you know what I mean. So, resist the temptation to give up and surrender.

Do you sometimes need to change or adapt in your assignment? Absolutely! Do you sometimes need to quit doing what you're doing? Yes, but I can tell you, the enemy comes with a spiritual attack to try to stop you or entice you to get off track to derail your life, especially when we are moving forward. That's his purpose, so we need to be wise and discern what is happening.

When a person is excelling in and accomplishing God's plan, the enemy looks at that life and doesn't like it. He doesn't want us to grow or succeed. So many times, he will inundate us with discouraging and disheartening thoughts to cause us to quit and abandon our posts. So be wise to his tactics.

3) Questioning Your Call in Life

The **third** sign that you might be under spiritual attack is you begin to question the direction and the call that was once so clear in your life. You live a spiritual life, you believe in what you read in Scripture, but you start feeling like you don't want to continue anymore. You begin to question the direction, question the purpose, or even question God's Word.

The devil tempts you with reasons to give up on the very thing that you were once so passionate about. You may question prophetic words that God has given you or start questioning the spiritual breakthroughs God provided for you in the past. You begin to say, "Well, I wonder if that really was the Lord, or was it just a coincidence?" When you are under spiritual attack, your very foundation will be shaken if you allow it to be shaken. Stand up against this mental attack and command it to stop in Jesus' name—resist the devil and make sure you are fully submitting to the Lord. Interestingly, we read in James 4:7 that you must submit to the Lord and His way before you can successfully resist the devil.

4) Temptations of the Past

The **fourth** sign you may be under spiritual attack is that you're drawn back toward old bondages. The enemy wants to enslave God's people again. We once were in sin and bondage, but God rescued us. The enemy wants to lure you back into things that have been in your past. If you were a drug addict, an alcoholic, or a gossiper—it doesn't matter what it may be—he wants to drag you back into it. The devil will use a previous life of promiscuity as a temptation to cheat on your spouse—something that's been in your past can be used to try to enslave you. After he draws you into the trap, he then brings shame and condemnation upon you, and it's a spiral that just keeps taking you down, down, down.

If you see any of these indicators, take active steps to stop and reverse them; you can't be passive. Make sure your faith is strengthened by reintroducing yourself to the Scripture and any personal prophecies that God has used previously in your life to encourage and strengthen you.

"This charge I commit unto thee, son Timothy, according to the prophecies which went before on thee, that thou by them mightest war a good warfare" (1 Timothy 1:8).

This verse tells us to "war a good warfare" against the enemy through the prophecies that have been spoken or given to us. You've been empowered and equipped to overcome the evil one. Place faith in God's promises to you!

CHAPTER 13

HOW TO FIGHT BACK

What are things you can do when you're in the middle of an overwhelming attack? How do we biblically and successfully continue to deal with these spiritual onslaughts? Remember, you must recognize it and acknowledge it—don't ignore it!

"God resisteth the proud, but giveth grace unto the humble. Submit yourselves therefore to God. Resist the devil, and he will flee from you" (James 4:6-7).

Let's dissect this passage. We are told to resist the devil. But, there's a prerequisite required before you resist the enemy, and that is to humble yourself before God. The Lord didn't say He was going to humble you; He said to humble yourself. What does this humbling look like in our lives? It's evidenced by obeying what we see in the Word and the Holy Spirit's dealings in our own hearts (these two should agree). Then we can submit to the Lord—to His plan, His purpose, and all that He has for us. This submission to the Lord truly is a way to fight back against the enemy.

Who's the Enemy?

"The thief comes only in order to steal and kill and destroy" (John 10:10, AMP).

It's so important to get this straight in your thinking: God is a good God, and the devil is a bad devil. If this is not understood, you will be robbed and live defeated. The enemy comes into your life wreaking havoc and trying to convince you it's God doing it to you. Make sure you realize it isn't the Lord! God has given us a way out. We have to align our theology with Scripture—agreeing with the Word of God. Of course, we can open the door to the devil by disobeying God or living a sinful lifestyle, but remember God is a good God to His children and wants to bless us with overflowing favor, while the enemy steals, kills, and destroys. So live your life obedient to the Father to have His blessings flow into your life.

I'm thankful that Evangelist Oral Roberts brought revelation to me on this subject; I remember being a young girl and hearing him talk about how God is a good God. And I'm thinking, "Really? Wow, that's a wonderful thing to hear." At that time in my life, I didn't know that. I was confused. Was He good? Was He responsible for the disastrous conditions in my life? Was He part of my problem? Was He the solution? Because of what people were saying around me, I thought God was mad and unhappy with me. Have you ever been there? Some of you are reading this and might be in the same place I was at that time.

I'm here now to tell you that God is a good God! This is not my opinion; it's the Word of the Lord, which is the eternal truth.

We Submit

> "O give thanks unto the Lord, for he is good: for his mercy endureth forever" (Psalm 107:1).

So, we can and should submit ourselves to God because He's a good God. He's looking out for us and has our best interests at heart. This knowledge brings us the ability to successfully oppose the devil. Some have told me they resisted the enemy, and nothing happened. That isn't what the Bible says. In this case, I would ask myself: am I submitted to the Lord's plan? Am I living surrendered to Him? This is the prerequisite to being able to stand your ground against the enemy. Again, it says resist, oppose, stand against the enemy, and he will flee. What some do when the enemy comes is raise the white flag of surrender, lie down, and give in to his attacks; but, we are to stand our ground. Based on God's promise, if you oppose the devil, he will flee.

Then We Fight God's Way

> Therefore, put on the complete armor of God, so that you will be able to [successfully] resist and stand your ground in the evil day [of danger], and having done everything [that the crisis demands], to stand firm [in your place, fully prepared, immovable, victorious] (Ephesians 6:13, AMP).

Resist the devil, oppose him, then stand firm against him—don't give in to his lies or schemes—and he, without a doubt, will go. He will run in terror from you. Do you know why? Because when the enemy looks at us through the blood of Jesus, he doesn't see a normal man; he sees Jesus. You, as a faith-filled person, have the authority to resist and stop the enemy's schemes! He's not looking at your size; he is not looking at your ability; he is looking at the ability of God in you. You must DO something and SAY something. You cannot give up when things are going wrong in your life, your family, on your job, in your church, etc.—you cannot give up. No! God said He will give you the strength to withstand the enemy, and the enemy will depart.

Stand Your Ground

> Stand therefore [hold your ground], having tightened the belt of truth around your loins and having put on the breastplate of integrity and of moral rectitude and right standing with God (Ephesians 6:14, AMPC).

We need to hear, acknowledge, and practice this principle, even when we don't feel strong. I've been in this position myself when I felt so weak, but I refused to lie down. I'm not giving up; I'm resisting. It's like sickness or disease in your body; resist it because it is of the devil (Acts 10:38). I like to read about Smith Wigglesworth. When he saw a person with sickness and disease in their body, he didn't look on that person, per se; he saw the devil attacking their body! And with great faith, he began to minister to them and break satan's power that was trying to destroy their body. Then people would receive miraculous healings.

We resist—we bind the enemy in the name of Jesus—we do all these things, but where we stumble many times is that we allow doubt in our minds, wondering if it really worked. The Lord is the One who enforces His Word in our lives. We are to agree with Him and stand firm.

"Having done everything [that the crisis demands],
to stand firm [in your place, fully prepared, immovable,

> victorious]. So stand firm and hold your ground" (Ephesians 6:13b-14a, AMP).

In times of crisis, we are to hold our position of victory that Christ won for us at Calvary. Don't give up but stand securely on the firm foundation of Scripture.

Drive Out the Enemy

> "And the seventy returned again with joy, saying, Lord, even the devils are subject unto us through thy name" (Luke 10:17).

I don't exactly know how it works—when I say, "In the name of Jesus, I bind this demonic power in my life and this situation"—but it does. I believe it, accept it, and become childlike in humbling myself before God's Word and its ability to attract God's promised results to me .

> "'And these signs shall follow them that believe; in My name shall they cast out devils'" (Mark 16:17).

The Amplified version says, "They will drive out the demons" (Mark 16:17, AMPC). "In My name"—this is Jesus Himself talking here. So, this gives us another key that we can use when we encounter the workings of the devil. You're not on a hunt or chase for the enemy, but when you find him at work, you are to deal with him. Don't turn your head and look away and act as though you're unaware of his workings. Instead, handle the situation by driving him out. Then go on about your business.

When we are under a spiritual attack or when someone we love is under spiritual attack, we can deal with the devil and cast him out by fighting back. But this fight and victory occur not in our own name, not in our own might, nor in our own authority, but through the name and authority of Jesus Christ.

It's not a hit or miss proposition. I believe that when I speak the Word of God, the enemy has no choice but to listen and scatter. The enemy sees Jesus in me when I make this stand. I told you earlier about my appliances breaking down all at one time, did the devil stop his attack because I was mad or upset? No. My thoughts were, "We've not started this new church for the Lord and then stand back and allow our possessions to be destroyed to cause more financial pressure!" My thoughts and words to the enemy were: "I recognize you, and I see you for what you are doing. I cast you out in Jesus' name and command you to go."

You can bind the devil in your own life. Let me be clear here, you can also help others if they're open to ministry, but the only person that you have full authority over is yourself! You, of course, have authority as a parent of small children, but when your children get older and make their own decisions as adults, you cannot control or supersede their will—God doesn't either!

Stand in the Gap

You can have spiritual influence with others by continuing to pray for them. The Holy Spirit will deal with them, but you cannot make people do things you want them to do, or even what they should do.

Sometimes we get off course and stop believing the Word of God when things don't work out concerning someone for whom we are praying. Then we say the Scripture didn't produce. Many times, it doesn't work because we are trying to take a principle of faith that is meant for us as individuals and apply it to someone's life that we love or care about, but we cannot force a person to accept the Truth. The Bible says that we are to have faith for ourselves! Through our faith, we can influence, help, and believe for others, but ultimately, it is up to the person for whom we're praying or ministering to determine what they are going to do with their life. Our job is to continue standing in the gap and believing God to open their eyes. Certainly, we can use faith for ourselves, but our faith works differently when helping others. Knowing this will save much heartache.

I've known people who got addicted to prescription or illegal drugs. You can do everything you can to help them get free, but they ultimately must desire to be free. As we continue standing in the gap for these people while interceding in prayer, the Holy Spirit will continue to deal with them; He will give them every opportunity to receive freedom from the control of drugs or other entrapments.

People may not be making wise decisions in handling their finances. They might be prompted by the Lord or hear biblical teaching that instructs them on how to make wiser choices, but they don't heed it. They ignore it, push it to the back of their thinking, and keep going, living, and spending in the same way. Then eventually, they find themselves in financial trouble or even ruin. This is not God's doing or His will, but a person's own choice. You can pray for them to overcome harmful financial habits, but you cannot make them change. Over the years, my experience has been that when individuals who are financially failing find out what the Bible says about wise stewardship and put it to work in their lives, it radically changes their situation. They become stable and increase in the financial realm.

These are ways to fight back and not just accept things as they happen in your life. God makes a difference for His people, but they are to follow His ways to achieve His solutions.

Chapter 14

STRENGTH TO CONTINUE

When trouble comes knocking at the door of your life, it is possible to arm yourself to be able to stand strong against it spiritually. The Bible talks about an evil day that comes to everyone at some point, and we are told to stand and maintain our ground.

> Therefore put on the full armor of God, so that when the day of evil comes, you may be able to stand your ground, and after you have done everything, to stand (Ephesians 6:13, NIV).

Standing your ground is taking the position God has given you as a believer in Jesus Christ, which enables so you are not overwhelmed when trying times are at hand.

You may think the evil day will not come your way, and I would like to tell you that it won't happen, but the evil day comes at one time or another to everyone living on the face of the earth. Trouble comes knocking at our door, and we have to make a decision about how we are going to answer back when it does. How will we respond? How will we react? What will we say? What's going to come out of our mouths? Sometimes, we may even surprise ourselves concerning what we speak when the pressure is on. Have you ever been in a situation where you say, "Where did what I just said come from?" It will either be words of faith or not. It can be unbelief and cursing concerning where you find yourself, or it can be the Word of God that bursts out of your spirit. What you put into your spirit is what's coming out when we face struggles.

If we spend our days and hours placing into our minds and spirits everything that has only to do with this earthly life, we will absolutely not be ready to handle trouble. We have to make time for the Lord in our lives daily. Then when problems do occur, we can know that what flows out of us will be directed through the channel of our faith in God, His Word, and His ability. The Bible is directly where our strength lies—it is the incredible two-edged sword that is going to bring down the powers of the enemy that are forcefully working against us.

When difficulty comes, we also have to ask ourselves: will we become bitter, or will we emerge better at the end of the process. Some may even become bitter toward God because they feel He allowed the situation to occur. As I shared in the dedication of this book, my father passed away when I was only 19 years old. I grew bitter toward the Lord because my dad worked tirelessly for Him in the church he pastored. I felt God did not treat my dad fairly in that he died so young, at only 48 years old. I also became upset and resentful toward anyone and everything that represented God to me. I am grateful I worked my way through this emotional time by finally realizing God was not my problem; He was my solution! My eyes were opened to His truths, and then understanding and enlightenment came to me. Don't run away from the Lord if you're wounded, hurt, and lack understanding. Run to Him, and He will heal your brokenness and bring you wisdom and insight.

When we don't understand, we may want to lash out and blame others for what we are going through because our pain is so great. We may not know scriptural principles that would obliterate our faulty thinking. However, we must see the situation in light of the Word and handle it His way. I want to make it clear: God will help you as you go through the process of working through your trouble. You are not alone. You may say, "But you don't understand." No, I don't, but God does. He loves you, and He will help you and strengthen you if you allow Him. He has made a way out of where you find yourself today. You are going to make it!

Like everyone, I've had trouble in my own life. But I have good news for you—we overcome! Sometimes, we may not feel like it, but we need to act in faith (true faith is an action). You act, then the feelings will come. It takes child-like faith in the time of difficulty to receive the help and strength you need. Faith is the activating force in a believer's life upon which God moves. Will we get stronger, or will we grow weaker? You may not know it, but some decisions are totally in our hands. Give up or receive strength to fight forward. Make a conscious choice to see and approach life God's way.

I can tell you in times of distress, you might be weakened at that moment in time, but God can reveal in you His great strength. When we are weak in ourselves, He is strong in us. God excels at giving us His strength to overcome whatever we may face; it isn't in our human power or might. It is so important not to sever the ability for His strength to flow in us. Will we give up? Will we quit? I've seen people who, when times of trouble came, ceased to serve God—quit coming to church, stopped reading their Bible, didn't pray any longer, and gave up. He wants us, as children of God, to never grow weary, give up, or lose heart. We need to purposely move through the fog of life and continue serving Him—even loving and helping people—even in our weakened condition. I implore you to listen to this because this is key!

In the compelling story of Job, he went through so much anguish and distress that we can't imagine any single person suffering so much. Maybe you know someone who has gone through many heartaches, and you wondered how they kept going. God said that when Job prayed for his friends, it turned his captivity. When he took his eyes off his own trouble and situation, God delivered him out of his problems. I think this is an essential point for us all to learn and apply to our lives. It isn't natural to do this—it is one of God's ways to help bring about His ability in us so we can progress and move on.

If the Bible means what it says—and it does—Job's story gives us insight on how to react scripturally when we are struggling; we must reach out to touch and help others! Our prayers or actions for others sets in motion God's power to turn our own circumstances.

I am not telling you something that I have not lived out myself. Shortly after my son, Marcus, left us, I desperately felt that I needed to do something to reach out and help someone else for my own self-preservation! I had to get my mind off my situation. I was, as you could imagine, devastated and dazed by the circumstances; it was difficult to make even simple decisions. I've heard that you shouldn't make big decisions for some time after you have gone through a loss, and I believe this!

I knew it was critical to be distracted from my loss and turn away from what I was facing. In those days, it seems I always wanted to be somewhere else—never happy, wanting to run away—but it wasn't possible to get away from it; at the next place, it was in my face at every turn. I was seemingly unable to settle down and escape. However, I decided to try to take my mind off my pain (if it were possible) and reach out to do something for others. Our church was in a time of "Summer of Service" where we minister to communities in the area. I chose to work with a team on a Habitat for Humanity® project. I made my way through the day, and when we were cleaning up, I began picking up things we missed on the floor. My attention was drawn to a nail laying there—twisted, bent, and unusable. Immediately, my heart cried out to the Lord, "That's me, Jesus! That's how I feel right now. My life seems bent and twisted to never be the same again." It spoke so profoundly to me that I still have that nail in my possession. At times, I will take the bent nail out to look at it because it reminds me of where I have been, what I have faced, and most importantly, where God has brought me today. Yes, I am forever changed, but I am not bent, battered, or bruised any longer. The Healer has touched my life and raised me up by His power. I will never go back to be the person I was before this tragedy occurred, but I like to think of how I have been touched by the Master's hand. I praise Him that He has been so faithful to me! Now, because of my experience, I am a person with more compassion and sensitivity to others who are facing difficulty and heartache. God is no respecter of persons—what He did in my life, He will do for you.

> We are handicapped on all sides, but we are never frustrated; we are puzzled, but never in despair. We are persecuted, but we never have

> to stand it alone: we may be knocked down but we are never knocked out! (2 Corinthians 4:8-9, PHILLIPS).

I have been knocked down and blindsided, but I never let go of my trust in God. Through tears, I have said many times, "I don't understand, but I trust you, God." So, the enemy was unable to knock me out; he didn't keep me down! Glory to God!

I believe if you do the right things God's way, then right things are coming back to you. When we're in perilous times, we need to fight. Realize you are fighting back when you reach out and minister to others who are hurting or have needs.

My husband and I knew we had to fight back in the situation we found ourselves with our son. We returned to our church after taking a much-needed break. On our first Sunday back, I could barely hold my head up; it was terribly painful. I had feelings of giving up—I did not care if I lived. Some of you may be in this situation today. But from our depth of despair, we found His strength, and we began to fight back even in our weakened condition. You can fight back, too! We didn't have the strength to do this of ourselves, let alone the energy to do it, but what we did have, we used, and God supernaturally brought His power and met us. That day, we loved people, we prayed for people, we ministered, we cried—our congregation cried with us. God brought healing and strength to us day by day. It was both painful and remarkable all at the same time. Can I say that everything is just fine today? No, I cannot. Honestly, until I go to heaven, I don't know that life will ever be "normal" as before. Now, I am living a new normal. It is different and not what I would have chosen, but I know this, I found the strength in God to go on and function when I didn't think it was possible. I'm here as a testimony to say that God is faithful, and He causes you to overcome and triumph in whatever you are facing now or will go through in the future.

You can make the same kind of decision I made. Are you going to give up, or are you going to fight? You must fight God's way! Don't try to fight in your might or physical power—it won't work because you are unable to do it on your own.

Shine Your Light

"And there shall be signs in the sun, and in the moon, and in the stars; and upon the earth distress of nations, with perplexity" (Luke 21:25).

So, people in the world will face distress of all kinds seemingly with no answers or solutions. In 2 Timothy 3, it says perilous times will come upon the earth. A perilous time is a dangerous, stressful, and troublesome period that is released on our planet. In the middle of this perilous time, Isaiah speaks:

> Arise, shine; for thy light is come, and the glory of the Lord is risen upon thee. For, behold, the darkness shall cover the earth, and gross darkness the people: but the Lord shall arise upon thee, and his glory shall be seen upon thee (Isaiah 60:1-2).

When perilous times come, allow His light to shine through your life for someone else. We are told in Isaiah that darkness will be on the earth and "gross darkness" upon the people. This is referring to severe mental depression and oppression that will be present in the lives of people. In the middle of this dark time, it tells God's people to "arise and shine." These are parallel events going on simultaneously—great light and great darkness. There will be trouble, danger, anguish, and distress upon the earth, but at the same time, God says He will lift up a standard against the enemy. Do you know what His standard is? It's not a flag; it's His people—you and me—if you're a born-again believer. We hold up the light of the glorious Gospel of love to a dark world—to those who are hurting. We are the people of God, and we come out of trouble! We are the Lord's light pointing the way for others in that we have come through difficult times, and they can also. We went through the fire with God's delivering hand, and we don't even smell of smoke!

In troublesome times, reach up to God for His healing touch, and after you receive His strength, reach out to others. I am not saying this will be immediate, because we do need a grieving period. Begin by praying for someone who is going through a trying situation. Sow seeds of love, kindness, and good deeds.

Chapter 15

YOU'VE ALREADY WON

God's Word tells us that through Calvary, Jesus stripped the devil of his authority and reduced him to nothing. When the Lord went to the cross and conquered satan, He overcame sin's ability to destroy us.

> "He blotted out the handwriting of ordinances that was against us and contrary to us, and He took it out of the way, nailing it to the cross" (Colossians 2:14, MEV).

In biblical days, when somebody committed a wrong, it would be posted on a pole for everyone in the community to view as they walked by, which would bring great shame. I believe this is symbolic of the cross Jesus hung on at Calvary; He dealt with the sin and shame recorded against us. I want to point this out because our failure to live up to ordinances, rules, and regulations has been destroyed by the sacrifice of Jesus Christ and the shedding of His blood. You have been freed from those failures. However, the enemy wants to bring them back to condemn us if we will accept and receive the condemnation. Scripture reveals, if you've admitted and confessed your sin to the Lord, it's cleansed and washed away by His blood; it's never to be remembered again. After sins are repented of and we experience condemnation over our past, it isn't from the Lord—it's from the enemy.

"As far as the east is from the west, so far hath he removed our transgressions from us" (Psalm 103:12).

Conviction power in our lives comes from the Holy Spirit moving in our hearts. When you're doing wrong, conviction comes, but He doesn't condemn and shame you. He will deal with your heart and stir it for the purpose of repentance.

The Scripture we quoted earlier from Colossians 2:14 reveals that Jesus blotted out the handwriting of these ordinances that were against us—our wrongs and sins—and He removed them out of the way, nailing them to the cross. In being nailed to the cross, the price was paid once and for all.

"And having disarmed the powers and authorities, he made a public spectacle of them, triumphing over them by the cross" (Colossians 2:15, NIV).

Jesus triumphed over demon powers on our behalf, so we don't have to be lorded over by the enemy! One translation of this verse actually says that satan was reduced to zero. It is important to realize, believe, and think the right way about this. Jesus defeated and destroyed the power of the devil's domination over your life. Then He gave you the victory.

Jesus disarmed demonic powers and authorities. He disabled, incapacitated, neutralized, and paralyzed the enemy. So why are demon forces so rampant on the earth today, and why are they still attacking Christian people? Because the devil is a rebel, and he's going to try to get away with whatever followers of Jesus Christ will permit, while all the time, the enemy has actually been disarmed and paralyzed as it relates to God's people. If we accept what our Lord provided, if we believe and place faith in it, and then we resist, the devil has no right to stay but must desist. Stand your ground, and don't be moved away from your triumphant position in Christ. Have a seat and pull up to God's table of abundant provision!

You Have the Power

After Calvary, when Jesus was raised from the dead, He gave us, the believers, power to withstand the onslaught of the enemy.

> And Jesus came and spake unto them, saying, All power (authority) is given unto me in heaven and in earth. Go ye therefore, and teach all nations, baptizing them in the name of the Father, and of the Son, and of the Holy Ghost (Matthew 28:18-19).

Jesus received the power and the authority, not for Him alone, but shared it with us as His followers. You are not powerless; you have delegated authority that is to be used now in this time.

Jesus is really saying, "*All this power has been given to Me, and so I'm sharing this power and authority with you. You are to take it and go into the world.*" When you're engaged in life, and you come under attacks—the principalities and powers are rearing their heads and taunting you—understand that you've been armed and equipped with power and jurisdiction through Jesus Christ. So, don't be deterred, don't back down or back up—know who you are in Christ and the awesome authority and responsibility you've been given. Then with humility before God and with fierce faith, take your position in Christ.

There are times when I am going through some horrendous attacks and feel the pressures and thoughts the enemy is throwing my way; however, in the middle of it, God begins to rise up on the inside of me. I may feel like a weakling, but I say, "No, bless God! In the name of Jesus, you're not doing this to me, devil. I see through your lies. I bind your power in Jesus' mighty name, and I drive you out." Then I begin to speak the promises given to me in the Bible that are appropriate for that particular situation. Faith then rises, and fear leaves.

The Name of Jesus

"That at the name of Jesus every knee should bow, of things in heaven, and things in earth, and things under the earth" (Philippians 2:10).

Jesus' name is above all names and is powerful and mighty. Use that name given to you to bind the power of the evil one. When you do, there is power in your words because you are cooperating, agreeing, and partnering with God. He stands behind you. The force of faith is at work when you begin using the Word of God to counter wrong thoughts that the devil tries to plant in your mind. The battle really is in the mind! The enemy wants to keep you defeated, and he will try by entering your mind and thought life. He wants to obstruct and keep you beaten down and discouraged if possible. But if you allow the Holy Spirit inside of you to rise up, and you begin speaking forth the power of God's Word—even if you don't FEEL like it's helping—you'll see your situation turn around because you have released a supernatural force—the Bible! It will begin to turn your situation around.

As God's people, no one can stop us if we refuse to be stopped; but, if you lie down and allow it, you can be stopped over and over again. I believe that in these last days, God is raising up a glorious church with people who are not going to be weak, but full of His demonstrated power!

"For whatsoever is born of God overcometh the world: and this is the victory that overcometh the world, even our faith" (1 John 5:4).

This world needs to see the power of God in operation. When Jesus was on the earth, He would heal the people and lay His hands on them; wherever He found the devil and demon powers, He would cast them out. The people were eager to receive from the Lord; they were coming to Jesus because He had an anointing on His life. It can be the same with us as His representatives and ambassadors today. There may be people whom you know and have influence with that call you when they have a problem. Why? Because they understand you have an anointing from Jesus Christ on your life. You believe and act in ways they don't fully grasp or understand; however, they desire it, they need it, and so they come to you. We not only receive from the Lord in our own lives, but we can help others in their struggles to overcome.

> No temptation [regardless of its source] has overtaken or enticed you that is not common to human experience [nor is any temptation unusual or beyond human resistance]; but God is faithful [to His word—He is compassionate and trustworthy], and He will not let you be tempted beyond your ability [to resist], but along with the temptation He [has in the past

> and is now and] will [always] provide the way out as well, so that you will be able to endure it [without yielding, and will overcome temptation with joy] (1 Corinthians 10:13, AMP).

We may be facing something that we feel is the worst of the worst. We may be convinced that no one else on the planet has ever experienced it or understands it, but that's not what the Bible indicates in Corinthians.

There is nothing that can come against us that hasn't occurred to someone else. It has already taken place in someone's life. The devil has no authority to go beyond what is common to man, and he cannot take it any further. Use the name of Jesus, plead the blood of Jesus Christ, and speak the ever-living, powerful Word of God to seize your authority and stand in the victory Christ has given you.

The Blood

In the recent past, some wanted to eliminate the mention of Jesus' blood out of the hymnals because religious people felt it was offensive. Why? The power in Jesus' blood is offensive to some, but to the believer, it is powerful and dynamic!

Years ago, when Ed and I were working with a group of young people in our Baptist church, we began to see miracles take place. Teens were getting born-again and filled with the Holy Spirit. We were having a mighty outpouring, and when I say that, I mean it. We were not just **talking** about revival—we **experienced** genuine revival.

We met for Bible study in the basement of the church. At one point, a mother called the pastor and asked for help with her wayward son. So, the pastor called us because he knew we had our Bible study that evening. He wanted to bring this young man to the meeting for our group to help pray for him. We didn't understand many scriptural principles, but we did know about the power in the name and blood of Jesus over the devil's works.

As we were in the middle of our Bible study, the door flew open; the pastor, this young man, and his mother entered. The pastor had the young man by one arm, and his mother had the other arm—literally dragging him into the room. He had been sniffing paint for some time; consequently, he had paint in his hair, on his face and body, and all over his clothing. While they were bringing him in, we were all looking at each other; we couldn't believe what we were seeing! None of us had previously prayed and ministered to anyone in his condition. We thought God must trust us, so we wanted to do whatever we could to help him. We started doing everything we knew to pray and cast out any wicked spirits.

Finally, we determined that the young man needed to be taken into a small prayer room off to the side of the meeting area. We went to another room and began to pray over him, but then suddenly, everyone inside and outside the room started singing, "*Oh, the Blood of Jesus, it washes white as snow,*" over and over. This young man dropped to the floor, going absolutely crazy. He abruptly stopped in the middle of all this, looked up at us and said, "Will you sing 'Will the Circle Be Unbroken'?" The demons working against him couldn't stand to hear about the blood of Jesus! There was power in the song we were singing! That night, this young man was given a new lease on life. It was a supernatural occurrence and was a part of my spiritual educational process that I shall never forget.

So, remember when you come under attack, use the name of Jesus and power in the blood of Jesus. Talk about it, speak about it, sing about it—place the Word of God in your heart and in your mouth. Don't allow the enemy to destroy your life! You have authority over him. When he comes your way and the attack is on, deal with it! You've got the name of Jesus, you've got the Word of God, and you've got the blood of Jesus. Stand in your God-given dominion.

Fear Not

When you know the devil is working against you, don't give in to fear. Fear is not from God (2 Timothy 1:7). We have all been in situations where fear tries to grip us and overpower us. Its purpose is to try to block us from receiving our answers and desired outcome. But if you'll withstand fear scripturally, you'll win.

One time I was praying over our city, and a being that looked like a creature of war appeared in front of me as a spiritual vision. The hair stood up on the back of my neck. I thought initially, "What am I doing here? I'm in the wrong place. I'm going to get out of this room!" But something rose up on the inside of me that said, "Nora, you're not in the wrong place. In fact, you are where you are supposed to be exactly. You are standing and praying against the evil forces of darkness in this city (my hometown of Knoxville, Tennessee). God is using you right now to withstand this demonic force, so don't back up and don't fear." So, I began to command that evil being "in the name of Jesus," and I started charging toward it. When I charged to where it was, it disappeared. Sometimes you have to be willing to do things even if you are afraid to do them. I believe a spiritual battle was fought and won that day. I'm cautious to tell this story because some people may not understand, and it may cause them to act foolishly, but it is a true story. So, my point is: do what you have to do even while you're afraid. Remember: you have already won!

CHAPTER 16

WIN THE MIND GAME

It's imperative to realize in life that you're in a powerful mind game where light and darkness clash. In times of spiritual assault, remember who the destroyer is—satan. God is the answer; the devil is the problem. There can be a war in our minds with thoughts whirling around to make us stumble. There are negative thoughts, evil thoughts, perverted thoughts—all of them can bombard our minds.

> Don't let the world around you squeeze you into its own mould, but let God re-mould your minds from within, so that you may prove in practice that the plan of God for you is good, meets all his demands and moves towards the goal of true maturity (Romans 12:2, PHILLIPS).

We must update our thinking in these times and meditate on God's Word—the solution to our problems—and not receive implanted devilish, contrary thoughts. Many people give in to wrong thinking when the mind games begin by automatically receiving them as their own, then speaking them out—agreeing with the thoughts. Don't ever believe you are a bad person because of the thoughts coming to you. Counteract them—answer back with what the Scripture says about you. Examples of such confessions: I am a child of God; I am accepted in the beloved;

greater is He that is in me; no weapon formed against me will prosper in its assignment—that's real warfare!

Don't be infatuated with the devil. Don't watch demon-inspired films, etc. You can pick up a dark residue from the spirits that you do not want! Just look at the lives of people who were part of that kind of movie and see what has happened to them. Don't play around with it—it's not a game. If you're watching and listening to things contrary to Scripture, you are opening the door to a wrong thought life. For instance, if you are watching things filled with immorality, perversion, violence, and fear, you are loading your mind and heart with things contrary to God's ways that tear down faith and your ability to believe God. These things will also desensitize and callous your spirit to the quiet voice of the Holy Spirit. I protect what I see and what I hear as much as possible. I will not knowingly open my ears, my eyes, and my heart to the world's garbage. Garbage in, garbage out! Sometimes things do happen and slip up on you, but just because you had a thought does not mean it's your thought! The devil is loose on the earth to lie and deceive people. The Bible says, "Take no thought, saying" (Matthew 6:31), so don't make a thought yours by giving voice to it. This Scripture details how you personally take a thought: by speaking it out of your own mouth. When I have a wrong thought, I answer back, "No! I don't believe that!" Try this yourself when you're overcome with life's problems.

You can have doubtful, unbelieving thoughts, but don't receive nor speak them out loud, but instead answer back with faith-filled scriptural words. In difficult times, you can be sure the mind games will be present.

When the enemy talks to you about someone you feel is against you or is not treating you right, a negative thought may drop into your mind about them, but you don't have any evidence of its truth. Don't act on it and fall for the bait. Answer back: "No! That is not what I think. I cast that thought down; I don't receive it. Love never fails, and love thinks the best."

Do you see how I'm answering back, not receiving it, nor embracing wrong thinking, but replacing wrong thoughts with biblical thoughts? Meditate on this vital truth: "Love your enemies, bless them that curse you" (Matthew 5:44).

Again, we must answer wrong, negative thoughts. Jesus did this when He had the wilderness experience in Luke 4. He was in a desolate place and was under spiritual barrage from the enemy. There was temptation—spirit, soul, and body—in the same way, this is what the enemy comes to do to us. Jesus understands temptation; He went through the same kind of things that we do. Every time the devil came to Him with temptation, He answered and spoke out against the temptation. Jesus didn't say, "Well, I guess that's true. That's the way it looks." When He was tempted by the devil in the physical realm to turn stones into bread after an extended fast, Jesus said, "It is written, man shall not live by bread alone." He was saying, "*You're not going to overcome Me through temptation, but I'm going to overcome your attempts to derail Me through the Word of God!*" We, too, are to answer wrong thoughts with, "It is written."

In this temptation, the devil continued, "*Just bow down and worship me. All of this has been given unto me.*" But again, Jesus did not accept the thought. He rejected it and used Scripture to replace it. You see, Adam actually handed everything God had given to him over to satan in the Garden of Eden. When the enemy said, "*All this is mine, and I'll give it to you,*" Jesus knew that was a partial truth, but He also knew He was going to redeem everything back for mankind through His death and resurrection. So, He said, "*It is written.*" Likewise, when thoughts come whirling around in our minds, we don't have to say it, we don't have to accept it as how it is or will be, but we do need to answer back to counter any ungodly thought.

> Ye are of your father the devil, and the lusts of your father ye will do. He was a murderer from the beginning, and abode not in the truth, because there is no truth in him. When he speaketh a lie, he speaketh of his own: for he is a liar, and the father of it (John 8:44).

The devil is the father of lies, never forget that. Don't think the enemy is going to tell you anything that is a 100% truth. He may mix together bits of truth with fabrication as he did with Jesus in the wilderness. Be aware; he desires to deceive you and pull your life off course. In these last days, there is a spirit of deception upon the earth. The body of Christ is being flooded with trickery and deceit, but we must discern it and resist it. God's Word is truth, and the devil's word to us is a lie. We need to protect and guard our faith during the time of the enemy's mind games.

"Casting down imaginations, and every high thing that exalteth itself against the knowledge of God, and bringing into captivity every thought to the obedience of Christ"
(2 Corinthians 10:4-5).

What do you think the word "imagination" means in this verse? It's an argument; it's a rebuttal. In other words, if God says something, there's going to be an argument. "Yeah, but... What about this... Look at that..." There's a rebuttal—there's an argument that comes to our minds when strongholds are working against us. Cast down those imaginations. When you cast something away, you hurl it; you don't clutch it or embrace it. You get rid of it as rapidly as you can, like a hot potato!

On my day off, in warm weather, I like to clean or touch up my back porch. It's absolutely amazing what collects there. I never know what I might find on my porch. One day, I had two squirrels on my back porch! I was desperately trying to get our beagle, Maggie, back in the house, because I knew if she cornered those squirrels, it wouldn't be good—especially for the squirrels! On those days, I go out there in my cleaning clothes armed with every cleaning apparatus imaginable with me because I'm in the zone: the cleaning zone! As I'm cleaning, I see all kinds of debris, including dead insects—and I cannot get those things away from me fast enough! That's the way we need to be when it comes to the work of the enemy trying to implant thoughts in our minds that are contrary to God. We need to cast them away like they're repulsive to us, not accepting nor entertaining them.

Paul said, "Casting down imaginations and every high thing." A "high thing" is a principality and power or demonic force. Those powers try to exalt themselves and their way of thinking against and above the Word of God by trying to overpower it in our lives! But God and His Word works through people. Whatever you do, do not surrender to evil forces trying to affect your thought life.

The Bible, which imparts knowledge of God, is the absolute truth. It is the guide by which Christians live. It is what He left on the earth for us and called it His Last Will and Testament. Do you want to know what's in your inheritance? You have to read the Bible to discover it! If you have loved ones that have gone on to be with the Lord and you're a part of their will, don't you want to know what's been willed to you? When God talks about things in the Word, there is insight, wisdom, and details as it relates to our inheritance from God. So make sure you know what the Father has willed to you. You can find it in Scripture! Actively pursue it and receive it.

Strongholds of the Mind

Psalm 140:7 says, "O God the Lord, the strength of my salvation, thou hast covered my head in the day of battle." When the battle is raging around you, the Lord has provided a guard over your thought life. There is protection of the mind available for God's people.

"(For the weapons of our warfare are not carnal, but mighty through God to the pulling down of strong holds)" (2 Corinthians 10:4).

You have been given weapons listed in Ephesians 6:14-18. These are not earthly weapons—they are spiritual weapons including the sword of the spirit, which is symbolic of the Word of God, and the shield of faith. Your weaponry also includes the helmet of salvation and deliverance which is symbolic of covering or protecting your mind. All of these can be used by you each and every day when needed to counteract the enemy's attacks.

A "stronghold" is a fortress; in this case, it's something that's built up in the mind. For example, there are certain areas of the country where evil strongholds have taken hold of people and dominate their thinking in that particular region. In that geographical area, the people have bought into or accepted certain demonic thoughts as normal, even though they are evil and contrary to God's ways.

God has given us the ability to overcome these strongholds. Overcoming them in our own spiritual lives can only be done successfully by following and obeying God's guidelines. His weapons are mighty because they function through Him. It's not by your own determination or power; it's not how you can grit and bear it. God's weaponry strategically pulls down strongholds. It does not leave strongholds in place, continuing to attack and control.

God has given us the ability to overcome these strongholds. Overcoming them in our personal spiritual lives can only be done successfully by following and obeying God's guidelines. His weapons are mighty because they function through Him. It's not by your own determination or power; it's not how you can grit and bear it. God's weaponry **strategically** pulls down strongholds. It does not leave strongholds in place, continuing to attack and control.

> "Now the Spirit expressly says that in latter times some will depart from the faith, giving heed to deceiving spirits and **doctrines** of demons" (1 Timothy 4:1, NKJV, emphasis added).

The Holy Spirit speaks emphatically here because He wants us to see and understand this truth. He says in the latter times, some people are going to depart from the faith. We are told further that people who now serve the Lord may backslide in the time of the end because they listen to seducing, deceiving spirits. How do these deceiving spirits enter? They plant thoughts in the mind that are not dealt with, and they take hold and become strongholds. Doctrines, referred to here, are teachings of devils—the devil teaches his doctrine. That is absolutely astonishing to me, and I did not understand this for a long time. There is the true church, and then there is another so-called church that is being deceived (Laodicean church in Revelation 3:14). They are departing the faith, listening to deceiving and seducing teachings being whispered to them, or to others who teach and give voice to that demonic doctrine; they are being stripped of sound doctrine. They are being led into error, and they don't even know it is happening.

We hear that all roads lead to God. It sounds so inclusive and tolerant that everyone will love each other; we'll have a lovefest, and Jesus is going to be so pleased. Absolutely not; that's deception. Jesus said, "**I Am the Way**" and "no man comes to the Father except by Me." A doctrine of devils and spirits of error can try to seduce people, even though it **appears** to be so unifying, kind, and loving! You really have to think about and meditate on this. It seems that deception is rampant today. However, you can walk in love and stand up for the truth of God's Word at the same time!

The way to avoid deception is to make sure you are grounded in the Bible. If you are, you will be stable and will grow spiritually. It doesn't mean you won't stumble, but you can be grounded. I know possibly you've seen people who have started acting unusually, and these strongholds we're talking about have led them astray. We have to understand that when these powerful seducing mind games are going on, there are evil, wicked entities at work. But again, we have all the power to overcome them—we don't have to be overcome by them. You have to cast away their baited thoughts when they come, and then capture and/or uproot every thought, which means you bring them into obedience to bow to the knowledge of God.

Seducing spirits can also work through someone in your life trying to deceive you. If something doesn't agree with Scripture, don't entertain it!

You can get through the attack no matter what the enemy throws in your path. If you think about what the enemy does, you will see that he lays a trap that is craftily hidden. It's like soldiers in the military who wear camouflage gear and conceal destructive devices being used against their enemy. The enemy wants to lay a trap for you and blend it into your path so that you don't realize it's there, and then you become entrapped by it. Don't be ignorant of the devil's devices or plans!

Chapter 17

THE STAND OF FAITH

"But without faith it is impossible to please him:
for he that cometh to God must believe that he is"
(Hebrews 11:6a).

This verse contains a principle we need to realize and practice if we are going to be successful in overcoming spiritual attacks.

If you're going to please God, you have to believe that what He has said in Scripture is the truth. We must replace the doubt and unbelief with faith in our hearts, minds, and mouths! Faith is what will bring the impossibilities to us. Things are going to become possible through faith. Faith in your heart is activated as you speak the Word of God and, through your actions, pursue what God has promised.

"And that he is a rewarder of them that diligently
seek him" (Hebrews 11:6b).

Our God rewards and compensates those who seek Him. As parents, we want to bless our children by doing good things for them and showing them kindness. That's what our heavenly Father wants to do for us also. We are to live our lives by faith, and through this, our lives are pleasing to God.

Hebrews 11:1 in the Moffatt's translation says, "Faith means we are confident of what we hope for and convinced of what we do not see." This verse defines real faith. Some say, "I'll believe it when I see it." Well, that's not what the God-kind of faith is all about—you cannot see it, but you're convinced it belongs to you! This is real faith, and you cannot please God without it.

Some people think that hope is walking in faith, but it isn't. You need hope because the Bible says that faith is being confident of what we hope for (Hebrews 11). We do need to be hoping, but let's not leave it there. Hope keeps your faith alive; it keeps you moving forward. However, you cannot have hope alone; you must have faith with hope. Your faith will bring or attract your hopes to you!

This particular Scripture says, we are to be "convinced of what we do not see." You need faith to stand and believe when everything seems contrary to what you are believing. In struggle or crisis, it is imperative to have faith in God to change what we are facing. With man, it may be impossible, but with God, it is POSSIBLE!

"Examine yourselves as to whether you are in the faith. Test yourselves" (2 Corinthians 13:5, NKJV).

This verse says to examine yourself. It didn't say for me to come to you and inspect your faith-life. The Bible says for you to take care of yourself by examining your own life. You need to determine whether you are actually in faith—believing in Jesus Christ and trusting God's Word—or not. Don't deceive yourself. I've seen this many, many times in pastoring; we put the Christian lingo to work when we're around our church family to impress them by appearing spiritual, but the minute we get away from our friends, there's no real faith working. Instead, we're acting and talking as if God's Word is unable to change our circumstances. This is not faith in God, His Word, or His ability to intervene and change circumstances. I've observed people who have lived this way many years, but with God's help, you can determine that you are going to be a person of faith! If you are fervent for God on Sunday, be zealous for God at other times also.

I was reading the story about the disciples on the lake when the storm came (Matthew 14:22-33). Jesus was the One who told them to get into the boat and go to the other side. It took great faith for them to obey because they, being fishermen, understood fishing on the lake, weather patterns, and dangers. So, when the storm came, they knew what would naturally happen. As fishermen, they could read the natural signs, but they decided to obey Jesus anyway. They got on the ship, started across the lake, and then the waves became violent. The wind and the waves tossed them around, and they became fearful. In your life, you may be in the middle of a storm now, but you, too, need not fear but follow the Lord and obey what He guides you to do. Under challenging circumstances, it is possible for you to hold onto peace and inner joy. This is both amazing and obtainable. He told them to get in the boat because He was taking them to the other side—to another place. In the storms of life, be quick to follow Jesus and get in this boat of life—you are going to make it! The winds may be all around, and the waves may be tossing you about, but hear Jesus' words, "*Be of good cheer! It is I; do not be afraid.*" Then He will take you to the other side and out of the storms and crises of life!

There are powers at work to neutralize your faith and halt the flow of faith into your life—the very thing that supplies, nourishes, and strengthens you spiritually. Satan wants to counter the effects of the Word of God in your life because he knows if you take the Scriptures and stand firmly on them, you're going to receive your answer from the Lord "come hell or high water." But remember, if the enemy can get you derailed by stealing your belief, he will further attack your mind and convince you that God caused your situation to occur.

I have learned you can always trust and rely on the Lord; He has proven that repeatedly in my life.

CHAPTER 18

CONCLUSION

What I have discussed in this book are things to consider when you're going through difficulty. These are principles I have learned that will change things for you—whether it's a challenge or some kind of life-altering event. God can turn things around, reverse the curse, and shift things from adversity to bring great victory. You cannot figure it out or even understand how it will happen. Only believe! Place these truths in your "arsenal" and use them at the proper time. Don't give up, but work the kingdom principles outlined in the Bible. Having faith in these principles is imperative. Believe them and act like they are true. All things are possible to those who believe! The impossibilities become possible!

Remember:

1) Everyone faces crises in life, but not everyone handles them in a way that overcomes.
2) Decide to think, talk, and act according to God's instruction from Scripture.
3) Trust in the Lord with your whole heart and don't lean to your own understanding.
4) When you're weary, weak, and drained, make a decision—seek recharging or renewal.

5) Have faith in the Lord, and His promises will move obstacles for you.
6) Drive out the devil before he drives out the fountain of God's promises.
7) Remember: God is good, and the devil is an evil liar.

The Bible says to trust in the Lord at ALL times. Sometimes we trust God until something challenging happens; then, we turn away. However, we must always lean on Him!

Bad things happen to good people, but it doesn't mean we quit! It doesn't mean that God did it. I must admit, there are times when I don't understand things, and maybe when I get to heaven, I'll have a better understanding. For now, though, I always trust in the Lord because He is on my side all the time. Remind yourself and reflect on this—in difficult times, you can overcome through God's help and following your instruction guide, the Bible!

I have shared my own experiences and the knowledge I have learned as God has faithfully guided me through life's experiences, I want you to know He will be there for you. In God, you will overcome!

ABOUT THE AUTHOR

Nora (Ramsey) King was born and raised in Knoxville, a city in East Tennessee—a gateway to the Smoky Mountains. She grew up the second of four children; her father, a Baptist preacher, set a godly example for her, teaching her to love and serve the Lord. Nora came to Jesus Christ at the age of 13, but never really lived for God until years later when she attended a Billy Graham Crusade and rededicated her life to Jesus Christ. From that experience, Nora began to learn more about the Lord as she read the Bible—a Bible that was given to her at the crusade—cover to cover for the first time, and she discovered truths contained there that profoundly changed her life. She has been captivated by the life-giving truths of Scripture from that point on!

She married her high school sweetheart, Ed. Their family grew with the birth of their daughter, Laren, followed by their son, Marcus. Early on, her husband felt God leading him into the ministry. Having first-hand knowledge of the hardships and challenges she and her husband would face—being brought up as a "preacher's kid"—they still wanted to follow God's path for their lives. Together they took a step of faith. Nora helped her husband establish a church while continuing to be a devoted mother.

During that time, Nora was sitting alone watching a minister on television late one Sunday evening when she felt the Holy Spirit speaking clearly to her heart the call to preach. She answered the call and was ordained into the ministry by Dr. Lester Sumrall. Nora and her husband also had the opportunity to be part of a small group of young pastors who traveled around the world with Dr. Sumrall, gaining valuable experience from his anointed ministry. She went on to earn a Bachelor of Arts in Theology from Zoe University and has pursued the study of Christian and secular leadership principles.

Nora has experienced difficult, painful, and challenging circumstances in her life, but she learned to trust, depend, and lean upon God. She has always found Him to be faithful. It was through the ever-evolving process of seeking and knowing God through His Word that Nora began exploring the depths of prayer. As she spent time in God's presence, her passion and fervency grew. She was drawn into a more intimate relationship with Him and began to experience prayer on a deeper level. She has seen the effects of the power of prayer resonate throughout her life and ministry. She not only learned about the promises of God and what He can do, but she learned how to unlock the secrets and mysteries of receiving from Him and acquiring what He had in store for her life.

Since her discovery that powerful and fruitful prayer is not complicated or difficult, Nora has shared these "prayer secrets" countless times in church services and conferences. She has traveled throughout the world, ministering God's Word with boldness and compassion, where hearts are stirred, provoked, and changed by the power of the Holy Spirit.

Today, Ed and Nora continue to work together as a ministry team. Nora co-pastors the church that she helped her husband start over 40 years ago. She has cultivated and still oversees and maintains the volunteer ministry teams of the church, which includes mentoring and teaching leadership and developing procedural training manuals. Her oversight also consists of church staff and pastoral care.

Nora King is the author of ***30 Days to a Better Prayer Life,*** a book that has been used as a Bible study guide and a daily devotional. She is also the author of ***Overcoming in Difficult Times***. The biblical truths shared in her books have reached across denominational lines to help people grow spiritually and connect more strongly with the Heavenly Father.

THE
PASTOR
NORA KING
PODCAST
AVAILABLE ON SOUNDCLOUD AND APPLE PODCASTS

edking
power of the word ministries

WHAT IS GOING ON?

Why I Believe We Are the Rapture Generation

Although the Bible tells us that no one knows the day or the hour of Jesus' return, God's Word does reveal solid information that illustrates how the signs of the times are lining up for His return to the earth. Pastor Ed King shares insight about the many signs appearing and circumstances playing out at this very hour.

Many of us will have the incredible opportunity to witness the second coming of the Lord Jesus Christ before we breathe our last breaths. But we must be spiritually prepared to welcome the Lord and be part of His coming kingdom, and **What's Going On?** can help all believers who desire to understand where we are in these end times.

ISBN: 9781973638872 • 298 pages • Westbow Press